Corruption at Grassroots

Public Perception, Experience and Victimization

Syed Umarhathab

Published by

Corruption at Grassroots-Public Perception, Experience and Victimization

Copyright © 2015 by Bonfring

All rights reserved. Authorized reprint of the edition published by Bonfring. No part of this book may be reproduced in any form without the written permission of the publisher.

Limits of Liability/Disclaimer of Warranty: The authors are solely responsible for the contents of the paper in this volume. The publishers or editors do not take any responsibility for the same in any manner. Errors, if any, are purely unintentional and readers are required to communicate such errors to the editors or publishers to avoid discrepancies in future. No warranty may be created or extended by sales or promotional materials. The advice and strategies contained herein may not be suitable for every situation. This work is sold with the understanding that the publisher is not engaged in rendering legal, accounting, or other professional services. If professional assistance is required, the services of a competent professional person should be sought. Further, reader should be aware that internet website listed in this work may have changed or disappeared between when this was written and when it is read.

Bonfring also publishes its books in a variety of electronic formats. Some content that appears in print may not be available in electronic books.

ISBN 978-93-85477-52-2

Author

Syed Umarhathab

Bonfring

309, 2nd Floor, 5th Street Extension, Gandhipuram,
Coimbatore-641 012.
Tamilnadu, India.
E-mail: info@bonfring.org
Website: www.bonfring.org
Phone: 0422-3928700

Foreword

Retnapandian T.

Every community in India is distinct; natured by its environment. It is a beautiful sub-continent, a country with several languages, religions, land masses, food habits, practices, communities with strong constitution to protect its people and considered world's largest democracy. With rich culture, natural resources and man power, the Indian Administrative System is unable to provide neither the citizens with corruption free society nor unable to produce people friendly public administration. As a result corruption is rampant; the conditions of corruption in India are different from other parts of the World. The act of corruption is widely spoken in India as evil; still not too many are interested towards curtailing it.

As matter of fact I should admit that every citizen of India is responsible for this situation. As a person working in the field of Anti-corruption for over 10 years I am unable to plot the causes for corruption among the Indian(s). While some of the important problems in public administration are well-known to everyone, still the idea of rebuilding the cultured society without corruption is a left dream on daily basis. While working on anti-corruption without research is absolute reason for failure to counter the corruption in India.

Dr. Syed Umarhathab was gracious to work on this area, which has least attempted in terms of empirical research in India especially at grassroots. His work is highly appreciable in a critical time where a new breed of young generation is preparing to face this world. This book will be a boon to the young readers to keep away corrupt practices. This book has elaborated on theoretical concepts of corruption and has successfully argued with empirical data, based on a research, wherein every aspect of corruption is inked, linked and deliberated. This impressive work will stand alone research document in Tamil Nadu for more years, because normally books are authored based on the reading whereas this work is supported with a research. This research is well planned and executed by a team of committed people. The chapters are well planned, titled, placed and prepared for better understanding of the audience. After reading this work I think that this book clutches the promise of leading us to a more responsible Indian society. I remain convinced that in the era of information, communication and technology, how a man is worried on corrupt social behaviour. It is essential for readers to not only read this book also to practice good observations and market this material to needy and policy makers in order to make good Indian communities. I thank Dr. Syed Umarhathab for providing me with an opportunity to read and gain the understanding of public views on corruption, their participation, victimization and experiences in fighting corrupt practices.

Retnapandian T., National General Secretary, Federation of Anti-Corruption Teams, Head Quarters, Chennai, Tamil Nadu, India.

Preface

Understanding corruption is important for several reasons. Corruption has infiltrated into all aspects of public life in India, making people lose their faith in democratic institutions. Corruption has been blamed for the failures of India as a super power in recent years. At the same time, corruption is viewed as one of the main obstacles to democratic institutions and open market economies. Yet, very little is known conclusively about what causes corruption to be higher in one place than another. The figure of the enforcement agency is unrealistic and does not show any real picture, an attempt has been made to understand the prevalence of corruption at grassroots, public participation, victimization, experiences, public attitude towards fighting corruption, and document the same.

There are enormous problems which spider the issue of corruption. This book is an attempt to successfully address the unfavorable condition that prevails in the contemporary Indian Administrative System towards reduction of corruption at grassroots. The positivity of people which was under-estimated in fight against corruption is disproved in this piece of work, as large number of public are willing to fight corruption but they are unaware of means to do? Whom to approach? Whether a reverse action is possible?. Hence, this attempt has highlighted issues pertaining to available public system and public senses/experiences at large. Hope the book underlines and has chalked out the gaps in procedures, practices and the policy, at the mid and low level of the public administration.

The aim of this book is to make reader aware of fellow citizen' s participation in corruption, their experience in fighting corruption and Governments effort to counter corruption at all level. While readers should not use the information for self rather, share in every place and platform for more dissemination of their reading. While everyone is blaming others for the corrupt behaviour that remains senseless, as quoted by former president of India Shri. Dr.A.P.J. Abdul Kalam that **"Fighting Corruption should start from oneself"** never look for others. When corruption is rampant, law enforcement should be pre-determined to weed it, as it is sowed. However, the ratio of reported corruption cases is far below than the actual incidences. This book presents public views on Corruption at Grassroots and has documented public perceptions, their experiences, interest, victimization and recommend suggestive measures to counter corruption at grassroots.

Syed Umarhathab

Acknowledgement

The first of my duty is to thank the Almighty for giving me a life and career in Criminology, then Manonmaniam Sundaranar University administration for funding the research under UGC unmerged Scheme and reasonable time to complete the same. I wish to express my sincere respects and thanks to my department colleagues Head, Professor (Dr.) P. Madhava Soma Sundaram, Ph.D., for generous guidance in several aspects and Dr. K. Jaishankar, Ph.D., Assistant Professor, Department of Criminology and Criminal Justice, Manonmaniam Sundaranar University, Tirunelveli for his constant motivation and supports during my course of occupation and support until now. I submit my sincere thanks to my research team Mr. K. Paramasivan, Ms.S. Gayathridevi and Ms. S. Jayasudha, for their valuable contribution during data collection and for their whole hearted support.

My special thanks are due to Mr. K. Paramasivan for processing the data. My sincere thanks to the Dean (Research), Professor (Dr.) N. Chandrasekar, Ph.D., Head, Centre for Geotechnology, Manonmaniam Sundaranar University, for approving funds for my research proposal. I acknowledge the assistance rendered to me by then General Secretary, FACT-India, Chennai for his valuable timely suggestions during conduct of the researcher and thereafter. It is my deemed pleasure to thank Mr. Edison, Librarian, AICUF, Loyala College, Chennai, Mr. Ganesan, Assistant Librarian, University of Madras, Chennai and the Librarian, Manonmaniam Sundaranar University, Tirunelveli for their support and kindness during the literature survey. It is prime duty to thank Dr. Shahul Hameed, Assistant Professor of

English, The New College, Chennai for reviewing the work and positive comments after vetting. I owe deepest respects to my parents. I will be failing in my duty if I do not acknowledge the contribution of my wife and children not only for their immense, unconditional love and support which they showered on me all through my life but also bearing my absence during the conduct of the research especially during the finalization of this manuscript. Last, but not the least, I thank all the participants of my study without them the data and this piece of work will have not successfully emerged.

Syed Umarhathab

Dedicated

to

My beloved Father and Mother

Al Haj Mohamed Gani V. O.

and

Al Haj Ansar Begum T. S.

For Grooming Me a Good Citizen

Chapter Contents Page No

CHAPTER 1

FUNDAMENTALS OF CORRUPTION

Corruption threatens the rule of law, democracy and human rights, undermines governance and endangers the stability of democratic institution and moral foundations of society

- Council of Europe

The world is witnessing growing, embedded, and systematic corruption, in every society. In all ages, prevalence of corruption can be traced in one or the other form. In most of the societies the issue of corruption is taken seriously and recorded- only the style, extent, nature and form vary from period to period and country to country. India being a cultural capital of the Asian continent has several panoramas in the approach to this social issue. Especially, an act connected with greed will be treated and taken in different forms by different groups. In some culture it is worth knowing the socio-cultural impact on the topic of corruption. Corruption means bribe to most of the people, at the other end there are two other major forms nepotism and misappropriation of the public property, which is seriously untouched as well unrecognized. There are several factors attached to the issue of corruption, still one factor is inseparable, that is development. While an economy is developing it will have a sparking corruption as part of its development. Corruption and development has intense relationship with each other, and grease the economy to roll in a normal spin.

Since 1990's India is working to achieve technological saturation giving minimal space for development in overall spectrum of the lives of the people. In an advancing society crimes are always expected to be rising (Chockalingham, 2003 p 117), especially from the interest groups (Buscaglia and Dijk, 2003 p 4), the greatest problem is higher incidences; the more alarming is the new form of crimes, their nature and unprecedented patterns (Jaishankar, 2007). Especially, the corruption endemic in our public and private institutions creates certainly an abhorrent scene, new forms of corruption cropping up make us shudder (Jose, 2010 p 37). India is sustaining to retain its position at various fields and levels with gigantic race over retaining the countries positions in global economy. Corruption is generally exhaustive in countries which are developed and developing, large or small, market-oriented or in some cases; whole political classes have been replaced (Samimi and Abedini, 2011).

Corruption is what corruption does, and its evil acts are both old and new. No honest citizens can point a finger only at the current government for the accumulated sin of corruption in India (Talukdar, 2012 p 30). India still retains the title of being in the big league of the most corrupt countries, corruption is one of the crimes that have, had, have been a problem for any society in this world; it affects the general morality of society (Umarhathab, 2007). Naunihal (1998 p 186) argues India has acquired the inevitable reputation of being among the most corrupt countries in the world (JhunJhunwala, 2006 p 11). Corruption is radically connected with government agencies or public sector at large; Corruption in India is entirely different from any part of the world as it is a multi- cultural, linguistic, religious, creed, and caste society. Any individual gaining something as a result of his/her action during his/her course of occupation i.e. as a public servant, go unaccountable as the administrative system in India has no control neither over such instances nor on the public servant. As in many countries there are several reasons for widespread of corruption in India, particularly among the public sectors. Corruption is multi-faced and complex, intervention on many fronts and the collaborative effort of many people are required to control it (Naunihal, 1998 p 191). There have been enormous steps to fight the menace both from central and state government, but result remains un-plaque.

Conceptual Definitions of Corruption

Corruption is defined as using public office for private gains. Generally corruption is "the abuse of entrusted power for private gain" (Transparency International, 2012). Two thousand years ago, Kautilya, defined, corruption as the misuse of public office for private gain, has attracted a great deal of attention in recent years (Samimi and Abedini, 2011). While Noonam (1984) defined bribery (corruption) as "the act or practice of a person benefiting a person in order to betray a trust or to perform a duty meant to be performed freely" while Bayley (1966, p 720) defines corruption as the misuse of authority for personal gain and not secluded to a monetary gain; any type of personal gain. Werlin (1973) simply puts it as the use of public resources for private activities. In contrast, Johnston (2005, p 8-9) argues and defines corruption as a consequence of the asymmetries of power and wealth that can arise from trading with the rest of the world and to Lee-Chai, Chen, and Chartrand (2002, p 45) corruption is abuse of power driven by intentional and strategic activities.

Other definitions have also been offered citing the misuse of public office, violation of public interest, disapproval of public opinion and the illegal use of public office for private (Vir, 2006 p 9). From the criminal law perspective the definition of "corruption" is not devoid of sociological or criminological orientations. Friedman (2002) has rightly remarked, the state of the criminal law continues to be a decisive reflection of the social consequences of society. Criminal law in particular is sensitive to changes in social structure, adaptability, class, acceptability and social thinking. However, it must be admitted that criminal law is although sensitive to social change and justice, yet it has not been able to keep pace with social transfusion, transformation or metamorphis, so as to cope up with the new challenges in the contemporary world for example the issues related to corruption. In nutshell, corruption is utilization of public organ for private ends -gains (Naunihal, 1998 p XLvii). To Jayawickrama (2004 p 2) corruption means the misuse of public power for private profit.

According to World Bank (World Bank, 2012) corruption is defined in categories. **Grand Corruption:** means corruption involving substantial amount of money and usually high-level officials. **Petty Corruption:** means corruption involving smaller sums and typically more junior officials. **Administrative Corruption:** means corruption that alters the implementation of policies, for example getting a license even if you don't qualify for it. **Political Corruption:** means corruption that influences the formulation of laws, regulations, and policies, for instance revoking of all licenses, and gaining the sole right to operate the beer or gas monopoly, for example the distribution of spectrum in India. Naunihal (1998 p 197) explains corruption as popularly understood, it is giving or accepting some kind of compensation in the form of money, office or position etc., for a service rendered in an illegal form, or by over stepping one's legal authority.

The legal definition of corruption in India is according to the section 2 of the Prevention of Corruption Act (1988) construe through Public Servant and Public duty, as

"Covering every person who is in the actual possession of the situation of a public servant and discharging public duty which the state, public or the community at large has a interest. Persons holding various public offices are public servants, whether appointed by the government or not".

It is a kind of reward promised or taken, or compensation expected for a service which is rendered even in the course of fulfillment of one's normal administrative or other lawful duties. According to this law corruption definition continues with different kinds, public servant taking gratification other than legal remuneration in respect of an official act (section 7), taking gratification, in order, by corrupt or illegal means, to influence public servant (section 8), taking gratification for exercise of personal influence with public servant (section 9), punishment for abetment by public servant of offences defined in Section 8 or 9 (section 10), public servant obtaining valuable thing, without consideration from person concerned in proceeding or business transacted by such public servant (section 11).

Forms of Corruption

Forms are basically a recognisation of the motivators behind the different kinds of corruption in determining ways to combat the problem. Corruption can be classified as **grand, petty** and **political,** depending on the amounts of money lost and the sector where it occurs new forms include **bureaucratic, parochial** corruption (to achieve status) and **Market** Corruption (for money). An event of corruption shall fall under three main categories namely **Bribery, Nepotisms** (favoring the known persons or groups), **Misappropriation of the government** (public) properties (Umarhathab, 2007), **extortion** is threatening or inflicting harm to a person, their reputation, or their property in order to unjustly obtain money, actions, services, or other goods from that person. **Blackmail** is a form of extortion, **embezzlement** is the illegal taking or appropriation of money or property that has been entrusted to a person but is actually owned by another. In political terms this is called **graft** when a political office holder unlawfully uses public funds for personal purposes and **patronage** (Naunihal, 1998 p 198; Political corruption.net, 2010), for most of the public, corruption means only bribe. According to Transparency International (2011), it classifies corruption into 3 major heads

- *Grand corruption consists of acts committed at a high level of government that distort policies or the central functioning of the state, enabling leaders to benefit at the expense of the public good.*
- *Petty corruption refers to everyday abuse of entrusted power by low- and mid-level public officials in their interactions with ordinary citizens, who often are trying to access basic goods or services in places like hospitals, schools, police departments and other agencies.*
- *Political corruption is a manipulation of policies, institutions and rules of procedure in the allocation of resources and financing by political decision makers, who abuse their position to sustain their power, status and wealth.*

Wahitha, (2011 p 82) writes forms of corruption vary, but it normally includes bribes, **cronyism,** nepotism, patronage, graft, extortion and embezzlement. Bribes come in all shapes as **sex, commodities, appointments, gifts** and most often as **cash** (Naunihal, 1998 p XV). Forms of corruption include petty corruption or **conventional bribery** and grand corruption (Jayawickrama, 2004 p 2). **Cross-border** corruption (Johnston, 2004 p 25) involving international interests, actors, capital and economic processes (both licit and illicit) is a potentially serious problem in affluent and developing countries alike, and raises important questions for both analysts and would- be reformers. The other forms of corruption include **division based on region, caste** and **language** are the other factors that have promoted corruption, nepotism, and patronage (Naunihal, 1998 p 184).

Some of the Major Causes of Corruption

In order to understand an issue in depth, the radical causes should be identified. Some of the important causes of corruption in India are

a. Lack of awareness in procedures in public sectors (Vittal, 2003 p 3; NCAS, 2004)

b. Poor regulatory framework (example Common wealth games scam)

c. Lack of public will (Umarhathab, 2007; Umarhathab and Sivakumar, 2009)

d. Exclusivist process of decision making (example Common Wealth Games Scam)

e. Unimproved social system and social acceptability (Kalshian, 2004 p 5)

f. Dysfunctional legal system (Eigen, 2004 p 13) and discretion power of the judiciary(Naunihal, 1998; Balasubramaniam, 2011 p 6)

g. Official Secrecy (Vian, Brinkerhoff, Feeley, Salomon and Vien, 2012)

h. Informal payments

i. Globalization (Eigen, 2004 p 13)

j. Procurement corruption (Vian et al, 2012)

k. Traditional rural society (Eigen, 2004 p 13)

l. Rigid bureaucratic structures and processes

m. The transition hierarchical society (Eigen, 2004 p 13)

n. Absence of effective internal control mechanism and failure of citizenship (Naunchal, 1998, p19)

o. Dilatory administrative procedures and practices (Vittal, 2003;NCAS, 2004)

p. Public tolerance (Vian et al, 2012)

q. Absence of a formal system

r. The lack of values (Vian et al, 2012)

s.   The lack of ethics among the public servants

t.   Integrity of the executives/administrators (Naunihal, 1998 p XLix; Appointment of the Central Vigilance Commissioner in the year 2011)

u.   Lack of administrative accountability (NCAS, 2004)

v.   Cumbersome administrative procedures and practices (NCAS, 2004)

w.   Uncertainty of punishment (Naunihal, 1998 p XLIV)

x.   Lack of moral development (Eigen, 2004 p 13)

y.   Not entertaining local expert/requirements while making policy

z.   Lack of research/survey by the government and acceptance of academic researches and its suggestion.

High prevalence of corruption at significant levels, exist in India despite the existence of a relatively strong and stable governance, structure, institutions, law/acts, policies and anti-corruption agencies. The anti-corruption laws and institutions coupled with a strong oversight system such as the Central Vigilance Commission (CVC), The Comptroller Auditor General of India (CAG) and the Central Information Commission (CIC). But, some of the larger agencies are non-statutory hence, are like toothless snake. Indian administrative system has evolved over the years some credible agencies with experienced executives and enforcers. The interventions at several stages in a corruption cases have faded the anti-corruption system with an unrealistic value(s) entrusted with them. The original problem lies in implementation and there is a huge gap between the policies and practices.

Common Effects of Corruption

Corruption effects the general morality of society, it creates a black market immune from formal government control; indeed, it generates the "Black Money" that purchases the decision-making power of public officials. Corruption increases with all-pervasive expansion bureaucracy (JhunJhunwala, 2006 p 11). The result can be a criminalization of the entire political and bureaucratic system that further restricts the government's ability to enact well-intentioned and much-needed reform. Corruption seriously affects the economy at large, as it adversely affects the country's socio-economic development and achievement of developmental goals. It promotes inefficiencies in utilization of resources, import sub–standard material, distorts the markets with high price rise of the essential commodities, enhance ill- qualified products, compromises quality and quantity, destroys the environment and of late has become a serious threat to national security. It adds to the deprivation of the poor, discriminated and weaker sections of the economy. It creates large social issues such as social exclusion, indifference in growth of societies; rich going richer, poor going poorer, increase crimes, unbalanced benifit are likely to reach only influenced section of people. Saumitra (2004 p 9) feels bureaucracy should have deft talent from specialized discipline. Beginning with many public services including the executive of law, enforcers of law, judicial officers dispensing justice under social influence until polity, can all be described as case of corruption which affects the morale of individual (Naunihal, 1998 p 199).

Impact of Corruption

The impact of corruption is immeasurable, as it comes in several forms, categories, long and short terms. The major impact anyone can ascertain in a democratic country is directly reflected on the development, business, environment and governance. Corruption develops a social imbalance and directly impact on the socio-economic policies of the developing countries, is the biggest enemy of the developing nations (Thamilarasan and Venkatesan, 2011 p 84). India being a developing country concentrating much on the science and technology, over the years has lost control over its people's social behaviors, patterns especially on culture of its communities. The public policy and plan go unreached with $1/3^{rd}$ of the population hence; they stay below the poverty line. The ways in which corruption can manifest and impact on the economy are many and varied. According to the report of Global Corruption Barometer (2004) it has evaluated the extent of corruption's impact on three spheres of life in each of the participating country, on personal and family life, the business environment, and political life. But, impact is experienced in all corner of the society especially in the public procurements (Vian et al, 2012), which are activities highly prone to corruption and has serious impact on the several industries as well as society at large. According to World Bank estimate, the average bribe to obtain a public contract has been estimated as 10-15% of the contract value (Kenny, 2006 p 5).

Various attempts have been made to indicate the impact of corruption in quantitative terms, Kaushish (2012 p 1) writes according to world bank many government loses about Rs. 2 lakh crores annually due to tax evasion while about Rs. 40,000 crores is lost due to delay in projects. According to Union Budget (2012-2013 p 3) while it is a challenge to ratchet up power generation, the sector continues to suffer transmission and distribution (T and D) losses as high as 25-30%, on the other hand. The general relationship between corruption and inflation tax has been identified in some empirical studies indirectly (Blackburn, Neanidis and Haque, 2009). Hence, CVC therefore maintains a high focus in this area to reduce impact of corruption in India.

Theoretical Views and Explanations

Many theories of corruption have lost it validity as time passes, because human, morale, development and society changes are recurrent. Trocchi (1966, p 9) felt that theorizing is inescapable, and that 'the facts of the matter' are never something that can be separated from conceptualization or from politics. Various theories and researchers have stressed three aspects of socialization: the behavioral, the emotional and capacity to make judgments as essential part of decision making.

The behavioral- Rational Choice Theory is an approach used by social scientists to understand human behavior; it begins with consideration of the choice behavior of one or more individual decision-making units it is appropriate theoretical approach to corruption. McLennan (2000) argues about an emerging 'new positivity', which seeks to forge a stronger consensus about the state of the world and put the understanding to 'progressive and effective use in the public realm'. This 'new positivity' is not an anti-intellectual (i.e Rational Emotive Theory) trend that imagines it might be of an antidote, postmodernists decided to jettison the notion of universal truth in favor of embracing individual-level truths (McGettigan, 2008). Merton (1957) writes American dreams- implies the culturally prescribed means for achieving the goals that are not evenly distributed among all members and social groups in society. Cloward and Ohlin (1960) summed their views that availability of illegitimate means may not be evenly distributed among society. Adolescents growing up in neighborhoods with extensive informal economies might have easier access to illegitimate business opportunities than youngsters growing up in neighborhoods without these crimino-genic opportunity structures. Hence, the strain theory proved very popular in the explanation of white-collar crime, especially combined with the notion of anomie (Passas, 1990; Cohen, 1995).

The emotional corruption and the global competition have claimed a proportionate and judgmental aspect of moral actions. Naunihal (1998 p 204) believes behavioral criterion refers to conformity motivated from within, or simple resistance to temptation. Such a conception is implicit in the common sense notion, such of 'moral characters' as a set of culturally defined virtues, such as honest. The second criterion is the emotion of guilt i.e. self- punitive self-critical reactions of remorse and anxiety after transgression of cultural standards. Lack of clarity of regulatory requirements and therefore about applicable norms and the boundaries of acceptable behaviour is often seen as a typical feature of white-collar crime (Nelken, 1994; Zimring and Johnson, 2005). In their classic study, Sykes and Matza (1957) showed that delinquents adjust this normative lens by using techniques of neutralization that deny the seriousness of the offence and the blameworthiness of the offender is applicable to corruption. Is corruption a form of disorder behaviour? Ellis (1950) explains rational emotive theory that choice of disorder behaviour is a result of irrational and illogical thought process.

The capacity to make judgments and to justify, maintaining that judgmental standard to one self and to others. Some of the main theories of social change, in order to illuminate the connection between globalization and the dimensions of societal change thought to accompany globalizing transformations. This leads to the notion of 'development' and 'modernity' as prominent ways of conceptualizing global social change (Ojeili and Hayden, 2006 p 3). While the hypothesis of differential association is that *criminal behaviour is learned in association* with those that define such behaviour favorably and in isolation from those who define it unfavorably, and that a person in appropriate situation engages in such behaviour if, and only if, the weight of the favorable definitions exceeds the weight of unfavorable definitions' (Sutherland, 1949 p 234), this theory is appropriately germane to several forms of corruption.

Who is at Risk of Corruption?

The concept of corruption is ever ending in a democracy, where the system is rotten and which handicapped executives at large. The most affected people are middle and low income group; normally during their course of life they experience corruption at all levels in many ways. The mad race for quick acquisition of wealth, power and status in society made us ruthlessly trample under fort all those virtues, which once beaconed our way through thick and thin (Naunihal, 1998 p 183). Singh (2006 p 7) writes that there is a significant difference in patterns of corruption in India. The creamy layer of the government, judiciary and civil services is comparatively clean. It becomes murky in the middle level and it is rampant in the lower ranks of the services.

According to the report of the Global Corruption Barometer (2004) which shows that corruption hits the poor. In its survey about 50,000 respondents participated, half of respondents on a low income believed that petty corruption was a very big problem, while only 38 % of high income respondents felt the same. About one in ten around the world admitted paying a bribe over the course of the past year (Eigen, 2004 p 19). Corruption attracts at large middle class and mid-level public servant involving all point of time in life. In the view of the vehemence of corruption, there is a need for the amendments to the laws and constitution of the country, to specify steps for improving the working of the public institution with which citizens interact (Naunihal, 1998 p 191).

This chapter was dedicated for understanding fundamentals of corruption, and in the next chapter the genesis and continuum of corruption are discussed in detail with components, contentions and contribution from various indicators and factors of life.

CHAPTER 2

GENESIS AND CONTINUUM OF CORRUPTION IN INDIA

The concept of corruption should have emerged when human owned something for him or for their loved ones. While exact genesis cannot be traced still, the onus on corrupt activities can be compared with existing legislation or socially accepted forms of corruption. Its origin should have been when the first human wanted a man to protect him or his belongings. Hence, the corruption can be aged as that of human himself. To start with beginning of corruption in India we can trace through the Indian literatures which are undated. India has not been free of corruption from the day of its existence, whether in ancient times (back as days of Thirukkural, Puranas, Arthasastra or Epics) or the modern times (Pre and Post independence period), there are references of corruption in Indian literatures of all ages demonstrating forms, nature, extent, relevance, social acceptance and punishments.

Literary Genesis of Corruption in India

Among the Tamil literatures Thirukkural (estimated 2000 odd years as per Tamil Calendar) is considered a divine; it was recorder by saint/poet Thiruvallur (acquired name) with 1330 kural/ poem. It has 133 sub heads under three major head. In part I- under domestic virtue the matters relating to corruption is highlighted in fear of sin (21), ascetic virtue, absence of fraud (29), veracity (30), truth consciousness (36), testing of men for confidence (51), testing and entrusting (52) and in part II- under head wealth, avoiding fault (44), and on modes of action (70) is either recording or elaborating on the issues related to corruption (Cheyon, 2003). Another major literature is Mahabharat an epic, where King Dhratrashtra talked of justice and morality on every issue among his citizens but sided with the ill-designs behaviour of his son Duryodhan. The first recorded nepotism reference was given her, neither Bhishm Pitamaha nor Dronacharya, Kripacharya and Vidur ever uttered a single word in the Rajsabha but decried the acts of Duryodhan in private, which constitutes nepotism. Knowing about the consequences of ill designs of Dryodhan, their silence amounted to abetment to his ill characters. Same as treating well the guest and gift giving was the part of the traditional Indian society, especially among the ruling/upper class. Gift giving was a tradition in many villages, which never was considered a corruption, as the transaction is transparent and not secret; the scale is modest, not life-changing; the benefits are usually shared with the community, for example the council of elders; and the public rights are not violated (World Bank, 2012).

Corruption in Medieval India

It has been argued that corruption, in its most negative portrayal, is a western construct and what constitutes corruption and bribery in a developed country, is no more than a traditional and cultural practice in another. The corollary to this view is that where there existed traditional practices such a gift giving to chiefs and important people, this was done openly and with the expectation that the gifts would be passed on or shared (some view this as an early taxation system). The modern day practice of secret and personal gifts is perversion of such traditions and in many cases it is a modern construct quite unrelated to traditional practices. Even those countries that argue against the imposition of western values have explicitly recognized through legislation that bribery and corruption are not cultural practices but illegal and outlawed activities.

Corruption in Pre-Independent India

Corruption in India prelude even before the British regime, during and continues until, still there is no documentary evidence about corruption in India prior to East India Rule, but nobody can challenge about its existence prior to East India Rule. The first ever recorded corruption in terms of government in Madras (then Madrasa Patinam /Chinnayaka Pattinam) was building of **Fort Saint George** by Bartholomew Robins in 1750 (Leighton, 1902) and episode continues with number of cases increasing every year. The East India Company laid the foundation of both corrupt bureaucracy and parallel economy. First Governor General of India-Warren Hastings was notably impeached on account of corruption in 1787. During those days corruption was an underground operation where money was paid to do an **illegal act**. Also, it remained untouched or unknown until it is lighted. Of course corruption strongly rooted in India only during those days with a payment for doing an illegal act. The British rulers slowly were interested in imbibing the corruption in to Indian society and were successful even before the independence of India. Devarajan (2006 p 13) writes when the congress came to power in 1937 in six states, corruption was so rampant that Gandhiji out of disgust in 1939 wrote "*I would go to length of giving the whole congress a decent burial than put up with the corruption that is rampant*". Normally war leaves an irreparable scare during and post war, it was during the World War II when parallel economy got rooted as result of government control and private hoarding. Though during this period the black money made was only a small fraction of its present size, but the institutional and social practices, that would facilitate its rise, were developed then.

Corruption in Independent India

The official statistics on corruption by the Government of India shows a data which is unrealistic; still it erodes the value of India (i.e. **Truth Alone Triumphs**). The history of political corruption in post-Independence India began with the Jeep scandal in 1948, involving V.K. Krishna Menon, the then High Commissioner for India in London. Corruption charges in cases like Mudgal case (1951), Mundra deals (1957-58), Malaviya – Sirajuddin scandal (1963), and Pratap Singh Kairon case (1963) was leveled against the Congress ministers and Chief Ministers, left un-punished. Corruption in India has crossed all limits of tolerance (Wahitha, 2011 p 83). Corruption cases like Sugar Import scam- Kalpanath Rai (1994), Telcom scam (Sukhram 1996), Fairfax, HBJ Pipeline, and HDW Submarine deal came up since then. All the scams before the year1990 have been forgotten and remains faded.

Corruption in Contemporary India

The days have changed the style, the form and its modes have not yet changed, the 2G spectrum case is one of the best examples. D' Souza (2012 p 35) hopes and writes the worst form of corruption that public life can encounter is the undermining of the system of government which has been given by the constitution. All efforts of the government remain in paper, ventilating the days. Corruption has not left any part of democratic India as such. In some parts of India, the corruption is the key even to achieve the birth right of an individual, such as collecting birth to death certificate. The problem has entered the administrative system(s) of India, since independence.

Several mission and committees have undergone test of time but still no real time improvement is possible in the world's largest democracy. International organization like Transparency International conducts regular study on the situation of corruption among the countries and scores their Corruption Perception Index (CPI). According to CPI (2011) which measured the perceived levels of corruption in 183 countries around the world (Transparency International, 2011) India has been scored with 3.1 in CPI and ranked 95th corrupt country among the survey 183 countries based on 10 scales. While in the year 2014, India was scored 38 and ranked 85 among 173 countries. Still it does not give the complete picture; it provides a reasonable idea of the level of corruption in the country. Will this information help or reach India's anti-corruption measures, is another million dollar question!

There is absolute gap in understanding the corruption at mid and low level, perhaps instances at high end is taken seriously and handled carefully by the organisation such as Central Bureau of Investigation (CBI), Comptroller and Auditor General of India (CAG) or Directorate/Office of Vigilance and Anti-corruption (DV and AC) of the states. But the serious attention in midlevel corruption has not given any improvement to public hopes, who are not worried by the figures of high end, but largely on their personal loss what author terms as petty corruption. It is necessary to fight corruption at grassroots in order to fight corruption at high end because any issues which are untouched radically will never be eradicated successfully.

Corruption is cancerous and un-stoppable crime in India. It is diabetic in nature, which requires continuous monitoring of the disease with controlling pills, otherwise it spread or it may damage part(s) of the system. While this is tackled by number of laws and agencies, why is still continuing? The answer lies with number of cases reported to the agencies and action taken against them. Finally, the verdict of the complaint whether the accused is punished or acquitted, in cases relating to corruption the existing judicial system is beneficial only to the abusers. While it is a hot topic throughout India, why is there no change in the issue and its practice? To better understand the corruption in India it is necessary to look in to the available statistical figures at federal and state.

Will Statistical Figures give Appropriate Image of the Problem?

- India has good number of reported cases and very good number of unreported cases (Umarhathab, 2007)
- As a student of criminology we are thought and always consider reported to unreported crime as 1:3 ratio in general (includes most forms crime)
- Whereas in case of corruption it shall stale at 1: =>1000 even more
- In general, not all the reported cases are booked an FIR
- Many are withdrawn after a stipulated time for several reasons
- Threats play a vital role in withdrawal of cases.

Let us look at the statistics of corruption reported against public servant in light of the report of the Crimes in India (2011 and 2013). Corruption and Bribery of Public Servants are dealt under the Prevention of Corruption Act, 1988 by State/Anti Corruption Bureaux, Vigilance Bureaux and CBI with number of person arrested.

Table 2.1: Details of Cases Registered and Persons Arrested Under Prevention of Corruption Act

Years	No. of vigilance cases registered		Persons Arrested	
	CBI	States/UTs	CBI	States/UTs
2005@	827	3,008	NA *	3,510
2006@	719	3,285	NA*	3,425
2007@	610	3,178	NA*	4,531
2008@	NA *	3,371	NA*	4,295
2009@	NA*	3,683	NA*	4,218
2010	595	3822	NA*	4892
2011	600	3,613	56	4,062
2012	NA *	3531	NA *	4324
2013	NA *	4246	NA *	4345

Source: Crime in India, 2013

* NA means data not available

@ CBI is not supplying RDA (Regular Departmental Action) data since 2005 (Except in the year 2011).

Table 2.2: Details of Public Servants Involved in Corruption Cases

(Cases Investigated by the CBI)

Year	Persons reported for regular Dept. action	Persons reported for suitable action by Dept.
2005@	237	8
2006@	271	74
2007@	355	84
2008@	NA	NA
2009@	NA	NA
2010	294	87
2011	268	48

Source: Crime in India, 2011

NA means data not available

@ CBI is not supplying RDA data since 2005

- Departmental Punishment Nil
- Dismissal **None**
- Removal **None**
- Major Penalty **None**
- Minor Penalty **None**
- Categories of public servants involved in regular Dept. Action - No Information both (Gazetted and non-Gazetted Officers).

Table 2.3: Details of Public Servants Involved in Corruption Cases in the States / UTs (Cases Investigated by the State / UT Vigilance Bureaux)

Year	Persons reported for regular Deptt. action	Persons reported for suitable action by Deptt.	Departmental Punishment				Categories of public servants involved in regular Dept. Action		
			Dismissal	Removal	Major Penalty	Minor Penalty	Group 'A' Gazetted Officers	Non-Gazetted Officers	Pvt Persons Involved
2005	414	178	57	6	33	62	374	2	634
2006	677	177	78	6	61	60	217	2	621
2007	974	579	38	8	89	59	580	2	1,119
2008	736	489	53	12	106	97	269	2	753
2009	632	448	103	19	110	125	375	3	889
2010	1,134	801	60	55	116	129	50	2,866	953
2011	1083	637	98	24	98	94	383	2,886	1064
2012	1490	702	88	15	121	158	465 & 737 *	2996	1044
2013	1202	556	126	47	114	118	1631 & 643 *	3317	1071

Source: Crime in India, 2013

* Gazetted **Group B Officer**

The figures given by the National Crime Records Bureau implies little action against corruption. But, the quantified data proved to be irrelatively data, the event of corruption in a country where over 1.2 billion live. Altogether only 6500 individuals are booked by the central agencies and 2100 odds in state by state anti-corruption agencies/officials.

Statistics of State Invite more Unanswerable Questions?

For Tamil Nadu until 2007 details of corruption cases were published, from 2008 until date information is available only with either the police publication or the state statistical cell off late it is not available for academic or public.

Under White Collar or Economic Crimes, 2006

- Vigilance and anticorruption wing (PCA and IPC) 224 cases

Under Commercial Crime Investigation Wing

- IPC and PCA 116 cases

Under White Collar or Economic Crimes, 2007

Vigilance and anticorruption wing under (PCA and IPC) 227 cases

- IPC and PCA 91 cases

Painting an abysmal picture of the bureaucracy, the National Crime Records Bureau (NCRB) says more than 5,000 government officials were booked for corruption across the country in 2011. Ill-gotten wealth worth nearly Rs 61 crore was recovered from these officials. In the NCRB's 2009 report, Tamil Nadu emerged as the corruption capital with 790 officers booked. The conviction rate, however, remained low at just 34 per cent, with more than 1,400 cases put on trial in the country during 2009. Addressing a conference of the CBI and state Anti-Corruption Bureaus and Vigilance Agencies in 2009, then Prime Minister Dr. Manmohan Singh had said: "High- level corruption should be pursued aggressively.

There is a pervasive feeling that while petty cases get tackled quickly, the big fish escape punishment, this has to change (NDTV, 2009). "To be practical the need of the hour is mere the implementation of the existing laws, beyond this ethical- sensitivity and sensibility, dedication and commitment of the vigilance and anti-corruption bureau, it is their duty to protect and entertain whistle bowler and the victims" to report the incidence(s) of corruption. The corruption in a given society is measured and controlled with a fundamental cause and counter approach on the issues. Hence, to continue the next chapter we shall look in to the issues in fighting corruption and various relative variables in an elaborate manner, with context and contention on the topic of indispensible issues in grassroots corruption.

CHAPTER 3

INDISPENSABLE ISSUES IN GRASSROOTS CORRUPTION

Corruption is a global phenomenon capable of paralyzing a country's development and diverting its precious resources from the public needs of the entire nation (Umarhathab, 2011). While every nation tolerates a certain amount of corruption, the level of this abuse varies wildly across the globe. Corruption is not our exclusive monopoly nor is it a new phenomenon afflicting our administration. It was corrupt even during the colonial days and earlier and continues to explode, in India corruption shall be experienced by anybody in any form, at any time from birth to death. At least six problems are faced by every developing nations that are the political consensus, the corruption problem, the economy, debt, population and the brain drain (Hunt and Colander, 1999 p 412). There are lots of voice against these problems but only few are highlighted. For instances, the agitation against corruption has caught the mood of the country, but its leaders have not succeeded in going beyond! Corruption has to be dealt seriously at all levels. There can't be any single solution (Srivastava, 2011 p 21). Hence, Roy (2011 p 23) commented that there is a need for systematic improvements to deal with corruption at all levels.

Status of Corruption in India

There is no denying fact that there is widespread corruption in India. Petty corruption which affects the basic rights and services of the common man is highly rampant besides the grand corruption as scandals which break out every now and then. A report on bribery in India published by Trace International (2009) that states

- 91% of the bribes were demanded by government officials.
- 77% of the bribes demanded were for avoiding harm rather than to gain any advantage.
- Of these 51% were for timely delivery of services to which the individual was already entitled. For examples, customs clearing, clearing agent or getting a telephone connection, etc.

Fundamental Education in India versus Corruption

The fundamental education is compulsory until the age of 14; it has produced reasonable literates in India. For long years fundamental education in India was mere a simple and education of formality. Only after the year 2000 it has taken reasonable steps to educate the children. However, most of the fundamental education system in India does not concentrate seriously on morale, moral, ethics, values, honesty, dedication and commitments neither through thought process nor applied, the lessons are evaluated for marks and grades. From the beginning or at very young age every student is thought to be safe and secure, with the resources available and best ways or short cuts to score the marks/grade hence, students are corrupt at the very instance of the school education. For instances above cited social variables are thought at lower classes while it remains unnecessary; as it is not the right age to imbibe such strong concepts, rather the same variables should be made a compulsory subjects from class 8 until 12 for appropriate appreciation by the Indian students. What therefore required is a change in social attitudes and values, so that people will not perpetuate unhealthy practices just for false prestige or name, for which they have to indulge in unethical practices (Naunihal, 1998 p 200). Raj (2005) writes India's under development attributed to mistrust and dishonesty. As Frederick Keith Ross has said, corruption is a sin; every government denounces it and every government practices it. Pathak (2003) writes what do we give to our children? Let us make the children encounter true stories of honesty, dedication and selfless service on this corrupt world.

This situation calls for a long term measures. That includes, besides suitable improvements in the educational system, changes in the socio-political order of the nation and gets rid of the conventional educational system (Naunihal, 1998 p XLii). It is necessary to; restore the ethics in government servants as first step in reversing trend in which people, who see themselves as victims of corrupt elite, are increasingly stepping outside the law to survive (Jha, 2012 p 11). It is time we stop talking and discussing about values and ethics in class rooms, and start living it in our lives to bring changes in our educational institutions, organizations. Higher degree of trust and honesty, accountability, which results in strong human bond, higher will be the level of grown and development. As long as we don't emerge from our moral mouse traps, the corruption cat will look like a tiger (Thampu, 2003). For instance, the number of medical colleges has increased too fast over the last two decades. Many teaching posts are vacant, so there is no scope for selecting medical teachers with right attitudes. Many private medical colleges appoint teaching staff only notionally, full time indulge in private practices (Minwalla, 2003). Hence, this warrants the teachers and management to corrupt, it is up to readers to decide how the students of these institutions will be, and their morale, value and ethics will be of what? Even recruitment of teachers can be linked with Morale and Value of teaching community.

Is Corruption a Social Behaviour?

There are several aspects of our society and several short comings in our social structure, attitude and values system, which provide an impetus to corruption (Naunihal, 1998 p 202). Tackling the corruption which is a monster in a democracy- will require more than just shaming politicians. It will require changing the social hierarchies, social norms and the structure of incentives for politicians, officials, and citizens alike, because the world will not rid of corruption (Felix, 2011) consumerism and corruption are complimentary to each other, Naunihal (1998 p 201) writes consumerism is mere a trait of the middle class in India, there is very extensive middle class which will penetrate the minds of this class to be corrupt. The ability to distribute society's resources curb the abuse of power and corruption; guarantee every citizen is equal before law which is fundamental to a well-functioning society (Plathotham, 2011 p 20).

The very scale of spread of corruption has generated helplessness, at best, and apathy, at worst. These, in turn, tend to be rationalized in terms of cynicism or in argument that tend to aquiesa in corruption. Naunihal (1998 p 200) writes prevalence of several social evils and institutions, have added fuel to the fire of corruption. A good example is the dowry custom in India. The demand for dowry is increasingly affecting both the middle and lower classes where economic constraints are real. For those who make these demands, it is the quickest way to improve standard of living. Hence, it appears that corruption has slowly and steadily conditioned to be a social behaviour.

Is Corruption a Part of Human Psychology?

Human psychology is adaptable, if it is corrupt; it gives space for deviance. Human psyche is placed between right and wrong behaviour and motives. We are all susceptible to corruption in some form at one time or another in life. In fact, it can be safely said that the question of magnitude of corruption is directly proportion to the opportunity or situation one finds in oneself. Since corruption stems from the individual, the only solution of improvement lies with individual himself, a gigantic task almost impossible for the state to undertake (Naunihal, 1998 p 205). Human behaviour at times is complex and more sensitive. In modern days, globalizations at par with exposures, public have developed lethargy in them. Hence, people could not take corruption serious, also believes it is the way of life, if you want to enjoy life.

Bauman (1999 p 1) captures the ubiquity of the concept and raises globalization, at the same time, doubts about its deployment: "Globalization" is on everybody's lips; a fad word fast turning into a shibboleth, a magic incantation, a pass-key meant to unlock the gates to all present and future mysteries. Corruption has been part of human behaviour for several centuries, affluent globalization has changed its form, it is now the individual's purview to commit/ involve or not, hence, it is a part of human psychic.

Corruption versus Human Rights

Throughout the world, majority of the corruption cases are in a way or other, is a form of abuse of power. It pretends and give senses that corruption is absolute in public sectors. Kalshian (2004 p 5) writes corruption, in its most eclectic sense, doesn't merely connote a rapacious and venal leviathan: it also refers to excesses of the state against social and political rights of the people. Corruption violates human rights, undermines the rule of law, distorts the development process and dis-empowers the India and its constitution. The way forward is to increase the sway of civil society in governance issues (Kumar, 2005 p 6). When government of a country fails or neglects to curb or contain corruption that government also fails to fulfill its obligation to promote and protect the fundamental human rights of the inhabitants of the country in many respects (Jayawickrama, 2004 p 2). Corruption in a country at large violates the three important international conventions of human rights 1. International Covenant on Economic, socio Cultural Rights (ICESCR), 2. Covenant on Civil and Political rights (ICCPR) to which India is a signatory, and 3. United Nations Convention against Corruption, 2003 (UNCAC). This leads to the infringement of several civil and political rights including the protection of Civil Rights Act, 1996 in India.

Corruption versus Religion

No religion entertains the act of corruption, both are inter connected in India for several centuries, of late situation reversed, Naunihal (1998 p 203) estimates whenever religion and ethics come together, it is because both aim for the spiritual improvement of man. Among the religions this fact is more evident in Hinduism. But, then, more than being a religion, Hinduism is philosophy of life. The rich Indian culture, over the ages has stood on the portals of "**Dharma**" meaning duty. But, will this strengthen religion and its followers; over 80 % of the Indians are Hindus, but still corruption could not be defeated. The very basic problem is with the change in culture and educational system as whole, neither moral education is thought as part of the curriculum nor the religious. While India is a religious country how it has infiltrated is a Million Dollar Question?

Hence, values and ethics are part of education which is supposed to impart it students and engage them in some scared religious practices making them realize what life is and how should we live with it. No religion entertains corruption at any level may it be Islam, Christianity, Judaism, and Buddhism or any other. For example, a real time case of the Zapatistas, were in this way, they are able to attract a great deal of attention and bring international journalists and members of NGOs into the region, making it hard for the Mexican government to engage in repressive measures, and bringing into focus issues of political corruption and social exclusion, forcing the government to negotiate (Castells, 2000 p 190). They have very skillfully connected their struggle to those taking place elsewhere, in sentiments such as Marcos's slogan 'we are you': 'Marcos is gay in San Francisco, black in South Africa, an Asian in Europe, an anarchist in Spain, a Palestinian in Israel, a Jew in Germany, a gypsy in Poland, a Mohawk in Quebec, a single woman on the metro at 10 p.m., a peasant without land, an unemployed worker and, of course, a Zapatista in the mountains' (Ojeili and Hayden, 2006).

Corruption, Economy and Development

Indian economy is 6th largest in the world and it fares pretty well in some of the global competitive indices. In terms of the strength of the financial institution, business sophistication and innovation, we are among the first 30 countries in the world. According to a leading economist (Mauro, 1995) if corruption in India is reduced to the level of the Scandinavian countries, then investment would rise by 12% annually and GDP would grow at an additional 1.5%. There is no clear estimate of the global cost of corruption, however, according to the association of certified fraud examiners, all organization worldwide lose around 6% of the annual revenue to fraud and corruption (NCAS, 2004 p 23). Johnston (2004 p 25) writes cross-border corruption can facilitate, and be sustained by, illegal trafficking in money, drugs, technology, arms and human beings, this will create vacuum economy.

The significant damage corruption causes to the economy is development; it is felt strongly among the poor, and therefore contributes to enhancement of poverty. It usually threatens the social and political fabric of the nation. Corruption encourages competition in bribery and business rather than quality and price of goods and services. It inhibits the development of a healthy market place. Above all, it distorts economic and social development and nowhere with greater damage then in developing countries. Most importantly, the heaviest cost is typically not in the bribes themselves but rather in the underlying economic distortions they trigger and undermining the institutions of administration and governance (NCAS, 2004 p 23).

As with domestic corruption, weak and poor run institutions increase vulnerability to cross-border corruption (Johnston, 2004 p 25) and develops problem in security and safety of the people living in and around the border areas. Corruption in any form thus entails a conflict in interest (Naim, 1995). It can arise in government purchases, sale of goods and services, its regulation of economic and other activities with supervision and control of its assets and organization. On the other hand corruption and livelihood of the public are interconnected, which means the least corrupt nations are always the most developed and happiest place to live. Corruption is not only a western concept. In any society, there is a difference between what happens above board and what is under the table, of what is accepted and what causes outrage (World Bank, 2012). Endemic corruption not only threatens economic growth and social developments, but also reinforces the unequal distribution of opportunism and thus serves to undermine basic human rights (Editors, 2004 p1). It has been argued that corruption in fact could have a neutral impact on an economy and therefore, should not be illegal. Indeed some have gone so far as to argues that bribery can be an indication of high level of competitiveness between business and prohibiting businesses from bribing could result in them operating more as a cartel (NCAS, 2004 p 23). Corruption and development are closely associated with the lack of an established government; one that has inherent legitimacy is the problem of corruption. Corruption is the way of life in developing countries (Hunt and Colander, 1999 p 400). In a liberalized and free democracy, corruption cannot grow as well hard to eradicate. Corruption and poor governance are key issues facing developing nations today (Editors, 2004 p 1).

Corruption and Globalization

In this vein, there is some disagreement over the meaning to be attached to the empirical evidence used to support various claims about the effects of globalization. While some may argue that the 'facts speak for themselves', we believe that the available data must be reflected upon within a larger frame of concepts, interpretations, and socio-historical events. Ultimately, evidence about globalization is formed, sustained and contested within particular social, political, and economic contexts, and claims about this evidence must be assessed in light of this. Therefore, a new positivity implies the attempt to connect theoretical innovation and elucidation with substantive issues in the public realm – a return, in many ways, to the sorts of theorizing engaged in by the classical social and political theorists of modernity, such as Karl Marx, Max Weber, and Émile Durkheim (Ojeili and Hayden, 2006 p 2). However, the application of the strain theory is not restricted to marginal corporations. Since, all types of organizations are goal-seeking entities; innovative means to achieve goals –besides profit – can be used when conventional means are blocked. State Corporate Theory, explains in corporate crime, state responsibility was reduced to a lack of state regulation or a lack of enforcement (Box, 1983 p 64) or, going back to Sutherland, was conceived as belonging to the same social class (Sutherland,1961 p 248). It is the concept that has rooted since, 1990's and it is still acme over the years.

Corruption and Public Administration

The Indian Public Administration is old, with several patch in the system leaking from top to the bottom, hence there is systematic corrupt system for more than 3 centuries. Gibbon (1993 p 207) wrote "Corruption, the most infallible syndrome of constitutional liberty". We had a corrupt administration even when we did not have constitutional liberty. Objectively speaking, there is nothing wrong with the institutional fabric that we have woven for ourselves. If the policy has failed to achieve its goals then institution are not properly guided and headed (Naunihal, 1998 p XLiii). In a democracy, public administration is a sub system of the political system which by itself is a part of the larger whole called social system/structure. Holding the public servants responsible for much of their mischief (corruption), the people plead for tightening of the noose over them. They want that there should be a proper instituted system of punishment and rewards for them and also that merit should have an edge over seniority in-so-far-as promotion from one rank to another is concerned (Naunihal, 1998 p XLiv). Corruption is a symptom that something has gone wrong in the management of the state. Institutions designed to govern the interrelation between the citizen and the states are used instead for personal enrichment and the provision of benefits to the corrupt (NCAS, 2004 p 23).

Bribe takers are among the power holders in society; that is why they are bribed. In a modern society corporate bribers may be more powerful than officials they bribe. Muthukumaran (2003 p 7) felt these days, one often hears the statements that so and so is bold and daring to be corrupt, i.e. corruption is identified with daring, boldness and competence. Bribery is a crime because of its secret nature is likely to go undetected unless there is incentive to complain about it and a procedure for its discovery (Naunihal, 1998 p 12). Still, this system exists in state anti-corruption bureau and CBI, while safety of the whistle bowlers in unlikely. Some of the important cases such as; the high tech MPSC scam involving crores of rupees was unearthed because of a system failure (Rabade, 2003). Thakur (2003) writes coal India is going to fall one day, it will be because of rampant corruption.

Naunihal (1998 p 186) evidence both in centre and states of India points increase of corruption in the higher bureaucracy, a sizeable proportion of higher level civil servants are believed to be either corrupt on their own and/or to be acting as accomplices, conduits or agents for corrupt ministers.

In administration, declining ethical standards are seen more easily; corruption and various forms of bribes move the wheels of administration faster (p 204). The whole problem is that in today's fast moving world, the ethical norms are believed to be in clash with self-interest.

Corruption and Politics

Corruption in politics can be traced in several histories and sad path is that still it continues. We can compare ancient and medieval age rulers with contemporary politics as only the designation have changed. It can witness as every political party is behind a group, till date nobody has come forward with any plan to oppose the prevailing menace. Money buying power, money and black money, money laundering or corruption, Ali and Crain (2002 p 422) suggest-the effect of economic freedom on growth is independent of the level of political freedom and civil liberty. However, this conclusion is misleading since economic freedom is related to political freedom and vice versa (Hayek, 2001 p 15; Friedman and Friedman, 2002). Defection adds a dimension of uncertainty to the polity (Naunihal, 1998 p 209).

The analysis of corruption by various international institutions has led to the impression that there is a consensus among scholars and incontrovertible evidence that corruption is bad. It pretends that corruption became the escape goat for all the problems in democracies, as well in dictatorships. However, this conclusion is far from being researched or made logically acceptable. It is unclear what corruption is, what causes it and why still continuing in a democracy? In several countries blame game starts as corruptions are exposed. This seems to be part of an agenda of promoting smaller governments and liberalization.

The other end, it is unclear whether if corruption promotes economic growth or not. This debate has not been settled and there is persuasive evidence from both sides. This has been done in an effort to reconcile the fact that dictatorships and democracies experience both high and low levels of corruption. This is in a contradiction to the neoliberal ideal that economic freedom fosters democracy. Consequently, some institutions argue that corruption is a problem of individuals and more permissive cultures. Naunihal (1998 p 202) feels political pitfalls; economic failures and administrative loopholes have only worsened the situation of corruption in India. The soul-less giants oppress the workers and the consumer, pollute air and water, all environment, and corrupt those in political power in all the branches so that a high tide of people's socio-legal action alone can call to order these 'outlaws' (Iyer, 1984 p 30). According to Plato the ideal state was based on harmonious union of the three elements of reasons, liberty, spirit and appetite, in which appetite dominates (Naunihal, 1998 p 354).

In controversy to the above Indian experts writes information on solar mission not in public interest as large sum of the public money is being spent on JNNSM, non-transparency and questionable process of Ministry of New and Renewable energy are responsible for the lapse in renewable energy programmes (Bhushan, 2012). Men in India have not changed too much as in any other country for at least 3 centuries but mother land India has changed its ruling party several times. The time has changed many thing one thing that should not change and was entrusted not to change by the patriots and martyrs? On the political scene, the selfless dedication of the pre-independence patriots is missing for at least half a century. This may be attributed to the fact that the morality of purpose of independence being over, the ethical standards have fallen in post-independence era (Naunihal, 1998 p 206). For instance on the one hand the BJP want to support the Anna Movement against corruption: One the other hand, the party is supporting its leaders who have been indicted for corruption by investigative agencies and institutions (Dayal, 2011 p 26). Abey (2010) writes if you have been watching TV or reading news paper recently, you may have been left puzzled with news of how nation has been cheated of our Rs. 17600 crores. This is quite an unfathomable sum.

Philip (2010) observes the name Adarsh co-operative housing society fits it pretty well as it is truly an ideal of corruption. Thakur and Das (2009 p 10) indicates Jharkhand former CM amassed Rs. 400 crores assets. The popular wisdom holds that political instability is antithetical to prosperity well, not for all. According to DH news (2005) bribes for queries: parliamentarians caught on camera" corruption knows no pat business; they cover up of HDW, Airbus Scam (Puri, 2006). Naunihal (1998 p 188) comments corruption has been politicized just as politics has been corrupted in the sense that cases of corruption have been used for partisan political purposes rather than with any serious intent to objectively tackle the problem.

Corruption and Judiciary

The Indian Judicial System is so expensive, dilatory and inefficient that it takes years and years to decide on corruption cases while Vittal (2003 p 7) argues why won't graft flourish in a country famous for its judicial delays and poor conviction rate. The act of corruption is criminal and consensual; the victim are one who are not made aware of the arrangements as it affects his/her case; consequently, a number of acts of bribery remain secret and undiscovered (Naunihal, 1998 p XXVI). Balasubramaniam (2011) felt that judiciary was also sensitive to the issue of corruption in its. He agreed that the judiciary is accountable to itself. Earlier a verdict by a Delhi court convicting an individual for selling fake 'medical Degree' and gave a serious note to such matters. Later, it was detected that around 40000 such fake degrees were issued by him across the country (Gupta, 2007), where will these doctors practice, they live with us, near or far. Though this situation has been dealt cleverly by the judge still there was no clear warrant issued to bring the sold certificate. The caveat "**Law is Supreme**" in a democracy, it is necessary to have a judiciary to execute the laws, wherein their major duty is to give justice to aggrieved party, that to never promptly. The people's confidence in courts are reducing day by day, public belief of justice will be delivered in courts of India has maligned, as Indian courts have approximately 20 million cases are pending in Indian courts (Menon, 2009).

The punishment should be severe and certain to control the crimes. In case of corruption majority of the cases go unpunished creating no fear on the public servant, few cases are referred to the Regular Department Action (RDA) by the investigating agencies (NCRB, 2011). This gives the corrupt a leap and jumps or faces RDA with no guilty as the Indian administration is rotten. For appreciation of the above expression, the report of the CAG of India unleashed a storm. They are required to audit and review the telecommunication policy but, no one over period paid much attention to the CAG report (Cover story, 2011 p 16). Though the report delivered good piece of information on 2G spectrum distribution and its losses, it came so late that even 3G was auctioned by the time, was that a real delay or manipulated remains Million dollar question. Judiciary dealt with a great care but did not raise a concern over the delay in CAG report, its lethargy in reporting it directly to concerned authority for taking action. The issues came to light with the information gained by a RTI activist.

Corruption vs. Gift Giving (World Bank, 2012)

Giving gift was a part of custom and culture in Indus valley and Dravidian societies. Slowly as men developed he also added some flavor to spoil the love and sacred of those gifts. Later, it became covert, still the favor was attached to it, and today it has taken the scope of corruption. Although different societies have their own notions of corruption, here are four questions to help determine what is right:

- *Transparency*: Do I mind if others know or the press reports on what I do?
- *Accountability*: Do I report my actions to others? Do they hold me to standards?
- *Reciprocity*: Would I feel hurt if others did the same thing?
- *Generalization*: Would it harm society if everybody did the same thing?

However, corruption is what corrupt intention amounting to the act, it may have legal sanction(s). Still, corruption is against norms of any society in this world. In the next chapter we need to go through some of the corrective measures that are in practice(s), under the purview of both state and government of India.

CHAPTER 4

POST INDEPENDENCE AND CONTEMPORARY CORRECTIVE MEASURES

To deal an issue it is necessary that some mechanism has to be used, or some corrective measures need to be followed in controlling the menace. In general, democracy is lethargy and life is forestall to fight the system rather adopt the existing system. Hence, this chapter is fully devoted to understanding of the corrective measures undertaken in India with regard to corruption.

Some land mark cases of corruption, in the history of political corruption in Post-Independence India began with the Jeep scandal in 1948, involving V.K. Krishna Menon, the then High commissioner for India in London. Corruption charges in cases like Mudgal case (1951), Mundra deals (1957-58), Malaviya–Sirajuddin scandal (1963), and Pratap Singh Kairon case(1963) were leveled against the Congress Ministers and Chief Ministers. Corruption cases like Sugar Import scam (Kalpanath Rai, 1994), Telcom scam (Sukhram, 1996), Fairfax, HBJ Pipeline, and HDW Submarine deal came up. Since then and even before, in India, if government wants to drop out or mesmerize a matter it will constitute a committee on the particular issue, slowly the issue fade of itself/mildewed and in following years it will be dropped. In the independent India it is followed for every matter that ruling party feels unnecessary to solve or favor the alleged. Corruption is mission 1) Advice to a potential leader 2) Keep an open mind 3) Recognize the difficulties and 4) Maintain your idealism (Hunt and Colander, 1999 p 410-11). Unlucky some of the commissions have tested the times and hypothetically very positive and successful. As far as corruption are concerned some commissions have been formed, few important commissions are discussed as follows.

First Ever Committee in India- A.D. Gorwala Report

Under the constitution which came into force on January 26, 1950, stock exchanges and forward markets came under the exclusive authority of the Central Government. In the year 1951 Government of India appointed Shri. A.D. Gorwala Committee to formulate legislation for regulating the stock exchanges and of contracts in securities (SCRA). Following the recommendations of the Committee, the SCRA was enacted in 1956; it gives Central Government regulatory jurisdiction over (a) stock exchanges through a process of recognition and continued supervision, (b) contracts in securities, and (c) listing of securities on stock exchanges. It noted the chances of corruption in unregulated stock market. The materials of Gorwala report was one of the earliest (post-independence) official documents that lay naked the problem of corruption in India. Then owing to the public criticism, a committee on prevention of Corruption was appointed in the year 1962.

Santhanam Committee

During the last tenure Shri. Jawaharlal Nehru, then prime minister of India, appointed a committee to report the growing problem of corruption and to suggest remedial measures under Justice Santhanam K. in the year 1962 and same was reported to the Government of India in its report of 1964. The sudden extension of the economic activities of the Government with a large armory of regulations, controls, licenses and permits provided new and large (for corruption) opportunities (Santhanam, 1964 p 7). He writes "We heard from all sides that corruption has in recent years spread even to those levels of administration from which it was conspicuously absent in the past". Though its recommendation is still a vague, few have been taken by the government- To deal with high level administrative corruption, the committee had recommended setting an independent Central Vigilance Commission (CVC), bringing all public servants of the Central Government and its PSUs within its jurisdiction but keeping ministers out of its purview. Unfortunately, the CVC Scheme finally accepted and notified by Government by a resolution of 1964, fell far short of the Committee's recommendations. The basic weakness of this scheme, which is still in force, is that it has no statutory basis until 2003. Also, many other recommendations have partial been accepted and rest is yet to be touched by Government of India. Another important agency was CBI had its birth with the recommendation of the same committee in the year 1963 which incorporated the Delhi Special Police Established (DSPE) as the investigation and anti-corruption division.

In continuance, one such decision is creation of Lokpal. Even the later recommendations of the Administrative Reforms Commission (ARC) of 1966 to set up the institution of Lokpal to investigate alleged cases of political corruption against ministers at the Centre has yet to be implemented. Five times in the past (i.e., in 1968, 1971, 1977, 1979 and 1985) some kind of Lokpal Bill were introduced in Parliament but these were cleverly allowed to lapse. The sixth and the latest Lokpal Bill of 1996 is still pending in Parliament (Kumar, 2012).

Subsequently on the report submitted by Santhanam committee certain legislations earlier enacted were amended such as-Anti-Corruption Laws (Amendment) Act, 1964; Foreign Exchange (Amendment) Act, 1964; Prevention of Food Adulteration Act, 1954, Wealth Tax (Amendment) Act, 1964 and more powers have been conferred on the investigating officers and on the Magistrates for conducting the proceedings of the summary trials. As days goes lesser the spirit of such amendments. Now it remains as simply an amendment act(s).

Vohra Committee

A committee was established (1999) headed by then Cabinet Secretary Shri. N.N. Vohra, which came to be known as the Independent Review Committee (IRC), set up to study the problem of the criminalization of politics and of the nexus among criminals, politicians and bureaucrats in India. This report was very much in detail and reported the length, breadth, width of the core areas of the corruption with scathing tone how dismal the efforts to curb it, and recommended the establishment of a nodal agency within the Home Ministry to compile all the information coming out of the various investigative agencies. The need for improving the procedures for the constitution, and monitoring the functioning, of the intelligence agencies was also recognized by this report (Tummala, 2009). Many researchers have insisted on the specificity of the committee to tackle organised graft. Though the recommendations are length still, it is another commission without vision from Government of India.

Some Initiatives in India to Fight Corruption

Government of India in full swing was taking, tackling and handling corruption seriously still, it could not understand the means to eradicate corruption. It poured more power and enforces to fight the issue but still, never proved right. While it was more discussed at earlier stages of independent India later it was nevertheless a failure, because time and again members of parliament are alleged of corruption charges.

Emergence of Central Bureau of Investigation

The Central Bureau of Investigation traces its origin to the Delhi Special Police Establishment (DSPE) which was set up in 1941 by the Government of India. The functions of the DSPE then were to investigate cases of bribery and corruption in transactions with the War and Supply Department of India during World War II. Superintendence of the D.S.P.E. was vested with the War Department. Even after the end of the War, the need for a Central Government agency to investigate cases of bribery and corruption by Central Government employees was felt. The Delhi Special Police Establishment Act was therefore brought into force in 1946. This Act transferred the superintendence of the SPE to the Home Department and its functions were enlarged to cover all departments of the Government of India. The jurisdiction of the SPE extended to all the Union Territories and could be extended also to the States with the consent of the State Government concerned.

The founder director of the CBI was Shri D.P. Kohli who held office from 1st April, 1963 to 31st May, 1968. Now, it is an autonomous organisation in government of India, looking in to the cases of corruption, crimes of trans-border and trans-state nature and so on. From 1965 onwards, the CBI has also been entrusted with the investigation of Economic Offences and important conventional crimes such as murders, kidnapping, terrorist crimes, etc., on a selective basis. The SPE initially had two Wings. They were the General Offences Wing (GOW) and Economic Offences Wing (EOW). The GOW dealt with cases of bribery and corruption involving the employees of Central Government and Public Sector Undertakings. The EOW dealt with cases of violation of various economic/fiscal laws. Under this set-up, the GOW had at least one Branch in each State and the EOW in the four metropolitan cities, i.e., Delhi, Madras, Bombay and Calcutta. These EOW Branches dealt with offences reported from the Regions, i.e., each Branch had jurisdiction over several States (Central Bureau of Investigation, 2012).

The latest development with this organisation is emergence of National Investigation Agency (NIA). The new office is added to bunch of organisation and well taken up by the polity hence; its emergency has not brought any big change.

Human Resource in Central Anti-Corruption Agency

The total sanctioned strength of CBI as on December 31, 2011 was **6590** against which **5666** officers were in position with 924 posts lying vacant. The vacancies existed in the ranks of Special/Additional Director (2), Joint Director (1), Deputy Inspector-General of Police (3), Superintendent of Police (34), Additional Superintendent of Police (9), Deputy Superintendent of Police (133), Inspector (183), Sub-Inspector (143), Assistant Sub-Inspector (16), Head Constable (21) and Constable (124). The posts of 89 Law Officers and 40 Technical Officers at various levels, were also lying vacant (Central Bureau of Investigation, 2012 a). Here it is important to note that most of the positions are filled on deputation. While this department requires a committed work force, Government of India is yet to recognize it, hence the failure of Anti-corruption is witnessed and inspiration behind inception of this agency beaten.

Directorate/Office of Vigilance and Anti-Corruption at State

In pursuance of the recommendations of the Santhanam Committee on Prevention of Corruption, state governments were asked to form their own vigilance and anti-corruption unit for their state. The Government of Tamil Nadu constituted the Directorate of Vigilance and Anti-Corruption in 1964 and the State Vigilance Commission in 1965. A Vigilance Commissioner heads the Vigilance Commission. He advises the Government on the major administrative problems and prevention of corruption in public services in general and the manner in which an individual case of corruption that is brought to light should be dealt with. The commission has jurisdiction and power to undertake an enquiry or cause an enquiry/ investigation to be made on any information that a public servant has exercised or refrained from exercising his powers, for improper or corrupt purposes. It also has powers to call for any information from any department or undertaking of the State Government or from any public servant on matters within its jurisdiction. The Government of Tamil Nadu has set up the Directorate of Vigilance and Anti-Corruption (DV and AC) as a separate department as a first organised measure towards tackling corruption in public administration. The office DV and AC comes under the administrative control of the Government in Personnel and Administrative Reforms (N) Department. With regard to matters of enquiry and investigation against public servants, the reports on the result of enquiries/investigations are sent to the Vigilance Commissioner for further action. Sanctioned staff strength **748** and actual strength is **607** (Directorate of Vigilance and Anti-Corruption, 2012). Perhaps this department does not have officer on permanent basis hence, the very spirit of establishment of this agency at state, encourage a question whether it is necessary or not.

Central Vigilance Commission

The Central Vigilance Commission though created in 1964, became an independent statutory body only in 2003 by an Act of parliament based on a judgment of the Supreme Court. Its mandate is to oversee the vigilance administration and to advice and assist the executive in matters relating to corruption. It investigates cases of corruption arising out of complaints or detection by vigilance wings in the various departments and recommends punishment wherever required. It is then for the executive to punish the individual official.

Anti-corruption efforts were so far focused only on enforcement wherein it was assumed that strict enforcement of anti-corruption laws and punishing the corrupt public servants will have a serious deterrent effect. In the research area of penology there is an unending debt on whether punishment should be of certain or severe. This approach has not been effective because of the cumbersome process involved in punishing the errant and the deterrent effect is lost due to delay and dilution of punishment. Therefore having realized the shortcoming of an enforcement focused strategy, the Central Vigilance Commission is now proposing to lay greater emphasis on prevention, education and generation of awareness among the people as a more effective and sustainable means of fighting corruption, which is close to that of Indonesian experience, China and Hong Kong model.

Academics need to develop a sound preventive vigilance framework which would enable organizations to assess the risk of corruption and take steps to correct the policies, procedures, systems and strengthen their internal controls to eliminate the scope for corruption. An important requirement for the success of anti-corruption efforts is that it should be participative i.e. involve all the stakeholders and establish coordination among all agencies fighting corruption. These elements have been lacking so far in India for too long time.

Lokayukta

Lokayukta is the ombudsman institution of the Indian state. In 1966, a report by the Administrative Reforms Commission recommended the setting up of Lokpal in the centre and Lokayukta in the states, for the redressal of citizen's grievances (Laxmikanth, 2011). As per the Lokayukta act, Lokayukta means the person appointed as the Lokayukta (i.e. the institution and the head of the institution have the same name), who either held the office of a Judge of the Supreme Court of India or that of the Chief Justice of a High Court in any state of India. The very importance of Lokayukta was felt in every state of India, however only few states took the initiatives to form this agency as matter of prerogative. While in Tamil Nadu once in every five year the opposition party raises the need for the agency and left unachieved until date. Of the pervious experiences and researches, the role of private agencies has been underlined and its pivotal play in fighting corruption has been estimated, which is presented in elaborate manner in the last chapter of this book. In order check and ink public mood towards corruption and related matters, there is need for empirical data.

Hence, this publication will find and address the gaps at mid and low end of the public sectors or Grassroot corruption. An empirical study was conducted by the author to understand the public views, perspective, experience, participation and stress on the methods to combat and descript the reasons for public participation and victimization. In the following chapter the research methods of the empirical attempt are given in detail.

CHAPTER 5

PARTICIPANTS AND RESEARCH METHODS

In this chapter, a detail note on profile of the research participants, statement of the problem, research methods adopted in the current attempt to explain corruption at Grassroots is given for the readers to ascertain the empirical data of this work.

Corruption is a serious problem; it is widespread, deeply rooted, well-organised and tolerated. India is rated as one of the most corrupt countries in the world by many research agencies; the situation is also in favor, with unearthing of the scams every then and now. But, the figures of the enforcement agency are unrealistic; an attempt has been made to chalk out the position of corruption at grassroots i.e. Mid-low level public sector or agencies that are frequently approached by the public. Hence, author attempted to empirically study the gaps at mid and low end of the public sectors. This study would be an eye opener in understanding corruption at Grassroots by collecting data on the public perceptions, experiences and victimisation. This will allow the readers to view and picture the corruption at Grassroots. On the other hand author attempts to stress on the methods to combat and descript the reasons for public participation and victimization in matters relating to corruption.

Major Objectives of the Research

The major objectives of the empirical study were

- *To understand the public ranking of the corrupt public sectors, scams and the factors influencing their choices*
- *To catalog the participants reporting behavior, their participation and attitude towards corruption*
- *To check the awareness among the participants with reference to the government measures to combat corruption and*
- *To find out the role of media in above objectives.*

Area Selected for the Research

The current study was conducted in the 10 municipal corporations of Tamil Nadu which includes Chennai, Coimbatore, Erode, Madurai, Salem, Tirunelveli, Tiruppur, Trichy, Tuticorin and Vellore.

The following paragraphs features, what is a corporation?, brief information on each of the corporations of Tamil Nadu as per the corporation's official website, giving details of formations of corporation, total population, and number of literates for each UA/City, its staple occupation, total area in square kilometer and highlights, if any, according to the Census 2011.

Definitions: Towns/ Municipal Corporation

For the Census of India (2011), the definition of urban area is as follows; 1. All places with a municipality, corporation, cantonment board or notified town area committee, etc. 2. All other places which satisfied the following criteria:

- A minimum population of 5,000;
- At least 75 per cent of the male are working population engaged in non-agricultural pursuits and
- A density of population of at least 400 persons per sq. km.

The first category of urban units is known as Statutory Towns. These towns are notified under law by the concerned State/UT Government and have local bodies like **municipal corporations**, municipalities, municipal committees, etc., irrespective of their demographic characteristics as reckoned on 31st December 2009.

Brief Description of the Corporations in Tamil Nadu

Chennai

Chennai is the capital city of Tamil Nadu, largest corporation in the state and world's first declared corporation city. It consists of various migrants of Tamil Nadu and from rest of India. There are number of occupations available to public from self employment until investing in dream industry, employees are in great demand and many Multi-national companies have invested billions of rupees in their trade. The Madras City Municipal Corporation was inaugurated in the year 1688 (Historical Events at a Glance, 2012). The population of the city as per 2011 census is 7213895, with over all literary rate of (Men 86.81 % and Women 73.86 %) and covering an extent of 426 Sq km (Corporation of Chennai, 2012).

Coimbatore

Coimbatore city is the second largest city in Tamil Nadu after Chennai, and popularly known as Manchester of South India, situated in the western part of the state of Tamil Nadu. The population of the city as per 2011 census is 3472578, with over all literary rate of (Men 89.49 % and Women 79.16 %), covering an extent of 105.6 sq. km (Coimbatore Municipal Corporation, 2012). Coimbatore City is the district head quarter; it was formed in the year

1866. Coimbatore is well known for its textile and automobile parts industries and has excellent potential for industrial growth. In recent years it is emerging as a hub of software industries (Coimbatore Municipal Corporation, 2012).

Erode

Erode Town is the head quarters of Erode District, which was bifurcated from the composite Coimbatore District since the year 1979. This town was constituted as a Municipality in the year 1871 and was elevated to Special Grade during the year 1980 and upgraded as Corporation with effect from 01.01.2008. Since, it is closer to the city of Tiruppur and Coimbatore, the staple occupation is agriculture, livestock farm, cotton and cotton related industries. The Corporation consists of Erode, Surampatti, Peelamedu, Sarkar Chinna Agraharam revenue villages. The population of the city as per 2011 census is 2259608, with over all literary rate of (Men 80.81 % and Women 65.07 %), covering an extent of 109.52 sq. km (Erode Corporation, 2012).

Madurai

Madurai is one of the oldest city; the city Municipal Corporation was formed in 1971. It was announced as the Corporation, after Chennai, in May 1st 1971. It is here that the **father of the Indian nation, Mahatma Gandhi, started wearing only a loincloth**, in 1921, after seeing the people ill-nourished and ill-dressed. Madurai is famous for its Jasmine flowers, transported to most of the Indian cities and exported. 2500 year old Madurai is considered cultural capital of Tamil Nadu. Madurai known as the "Temple City" is one of the oldest cities in India. This city is famous for Arulmigu Meenakshi Amman Temple. This city is situated about 500 Km South West of Chennai, spread over an area of 109 Sq. Km. The population of the city as per 2011 census is 3041038, with over all literary rate of (Men 86.55 % and Women 76.74 %), (Madurai Corporation, 2012).

Salem

The Centurion Municipality was declared as the Salem City Municipal Corporation from 1.6.1994. The Salem City Municipal Council celebrated its Centenary in 1966. The city is famous for the steel and related industries with required man power trained in and around the district. Salem limits were further extended by the inclusion of closer Town Panchayats and 21 other Village panchayats with effect from 1.4.94, with an extent of 91.34 sq. km (Salem Corporation, 2012). The population of the city as per 2011 census is 3480008, with over all literary rate of (Men 80.7 % and Women 65.43 %). Salem is the Head quarters of Salem District.

Tirunelveli

Tirunelveli city an eight year old infant among the Corporation of Tamil Nadu; is a land which has so many laurels to her credit. This is a land of sages – much evident from epics and puranas. Christening of this place itself bears testimony to its antiquity and divinity. This is a land of freedom fighters as evidenced by the participants from militant patriots like Shri Wanchi Nathan, Veera Pandiya Kattabomman and revolutionists like Shri V.O. Chidambaram, Shri Subramaniya Bharathiyar, Shri Subramaniya Siva and others. This is the birth land of industrialists like T.V.S. Simpsons, Easun, India Cements – and also the origin of great News Papers like Thina Thanthi etc. This is the land that has perennial water supply through "Tamiraparani" – the only virgin perennial Indian River supplying water to the undivided Tirunelveli District.

This is the land that is famous all over India for its "Halwa" production and even known as Halwa City. This Corporation was formed by merging three municipalities' i.e Tirunelveli, Palayamkottai and Melapalyam and few Panchayat areas. The population of the city as per 2011 census is 3072880, with over all literary rate of (Men 89.66 % and Women 76.38%), covering an extent of 108.65 sq. km (Tirunelveli Corporation, 2012).

Tiruppur

Tiruppur Corporation, which is located in the Coimbatore district, is one of the most important industrial centers of Tamil Nadu. The Tiruppur Municipal Corporation was inaugurated in the year 2008. River Noyyal, originating from the Velliangiri Hills and flowing through the city center in the flowing through the city center in the easterly direction and the Western Ghats on the near west, are the major geographical features of this region. Spread over an area of 159^2 sq. kms, is the second largest town in the district of Coimbatore, covering an extent of 27.19 Sq. Km (Tiruppur Corporation, 2012). The population of the city as per 2011 census is 2471222, with over all literary rate of (Men 86.07 % and Women 72.07 %). The economy of the town revolves around the manufacture of hosiery and cotton products. The hot and dry climate prevailing in the region has been one of the various factors contributing to the growth of the hosiery industry in the town (Tiruppur Corporation, 2012).

Tiruchirappalli or Trichy

Tiruchirappalli or Trichy Municipality was constituted on 08.07.1866. The Municipality was upgraded as City Municipal Corporation with effect from 01.06.1994 by adding the adjacent Municipalities, Town Panchayats and Village Panchayats. The Tiruchirappalli City Municipal Corporation Council was constituted with a Mayor and 65 Ward Councilors representing each ward. The staple occupation of the district revolves around the ornaments making and agriculture. The many part of the river Cauvery flows and bifurcate the city, and is famous for the rock fort of South India. The population of the city as per 2011 census is 2713858, with over all literary rate of (Men 90 % and Women 77.24 %), covering an extent of 167.23 sq.km (Trichy Corporation, 2012).

Thoothukudi or Tuticorin

Tuticorin or Thoothukudi is a port town situated in the Gulf of Mannar about 125KM, North of Cape Commorin, Thoothukudi is also known as "Pearl City", it attained the status of Municipal Corporation in the year 2008. Thoothukudi and its environs form part of the coastal belt which forms a continuous stretch of the flat country relieved here and there by small rock out crops. The port hinterland of Thoothukudi extends to the districts of Madurai, Kanyakumari, Tirunelveli, Ramnad and also southern parts of Tiruchirappalli. This hinterland is a fast growing industrial belt of South India. Thoothukudi is a special grade Municipal Town. The population of the city as per 2011 census is 1738376, with over all literary rate of (Men 91.42 % and Women 81.77 %), covering an extent of 13.47 sq.km, a population of over 10 million (Thoothukodi Corporation, 2012).

Vellore

Vellore is famous for its rich history, town with the famous Vellore Fort and work ship places inside built as early as 1500 B.C. to function as one of the major seats of administration in the Vijayanagar Empire. Even in the modern world it is an important administration center being the district headquarters of not only the erstwhile North Arcot district for a long time but also the recently carved out Vellore district. The world famous CMC hospital with 1800 bed and 2000 daily outpatients makes Vellore as an internationally famous health center for more than a century. It is a major commercial center famous for the wholesale trade of rice and jaggery. The outstanding performance of this district in contributing to the Military service is commendable, as more and more men have enlisted themselves to the Military service, to serve the nation indomitable spirit and courage. A stone inscription in the building reads **"Vellore– from this village 277 men went to the great war 1914-18, of them 14 gave up**

their lives". The population of the city as per 2011 census is 3928106, with over all literary rate of (Men 86.96 % and Women 72.43 %), covering an extent of 87.91 sq. km (Vellore Corporation, 2012).

Major Variables of the Research

Dependant Variable

The dependant variable of this research work will be public sectors ie., government departments.

Independent Variables

The independent variables of the research are given below:

- Public ranking of the public sectors and scams
- Participation of the public in the event of corruption, victimization
- Reporting Behavior and reasons for corruption
- Awareness on the Department of Directorate of Vigilance and Anti Corruption
- Anti-Corruption Measures.

Research Methods

This empirical study was conducted among the public in 10 corporations of Tamil Nadu. About 100 samples from each of the corporations were explained about the research in brief and willingness was taken before the data collection. The sampling technique adopted in this empirical research was purposive sampling of non-probability sampling. The author (researcher) decided to collect 100 samples from each of the corporations, i.e. 10 corporations with 100 samples each is 1000 samples. Hence, the total sample size decided and achieved was 1000 samples.

A personal distribution questionnaire was prepared by the author (researcher) in the lights of the objective, which was finalized after the pilot study with the opinion and comments of the experts in the field of corruption studies. The tool was translated in to Tamil (Local Vernacular) in order to vouch the participants a clear expression, some of the participants were comfortable with tool in English. The pilot study was conducted with questionnaire prepared by the author (researcher), in order to understand validity of the tools with 30 samples in each district of Tirunelveli and Tuticorn. Later, author approached the experts in the area for opinion and the tool was altered and corrections were carried, comments and additions were incorporated, and tool was finalized. The data for the study were collected from the participants by the author (researcher) using a personal distribution questionnaire. The collected data were coded and entered in SPSS. The simple and appropriate statistics techniques were applied in accordance with the objective of the study; the results of the study are presented in the form of tables, combination tables, and diagrams as figures. The data collection was conducted for a period of 9 months.

Profile of the Participants

The profiles of the participants are important variables to understand the population of the research and their responses. The empirical responses are based on socio-demographic characteristics of the participants and reflect on impetus on the findings of the research. While in empirical research it is vital to read profiles of the participants in order to realize and recognize the results of the research. Hence, the author has decided to make it available for the readers to appreciate the profiles of the participants.

Table 5.1: Socio-demographic Variables of the Participants (n= 1000)

Options	n	%	Options	n	%
Age in Years			**Educational Qualification**		
<=20	137	13.7	Until class 10	74	7.4
>20<=30	463	46.3	>10<=12 class	143	14.3
>30<=40	212	21.2	ITI / Dip	48	4.8
>40	188	18.8	Graduate's and above	691	69.1
Sex			Other specify	44	4.4
Male	586	58.6	**Income in Rupees (Rs)**		
Female	414	41.4	<=10000	422	42.2
Marital Status			> 10000 <= 25000	392	39.2
Single	547	54.7	> 25000 <= 50000	143	14.3
Married	426	42.6	> 50000	43	4.3
Divorced	15	1.5	**Family Types**		
Widow	10	1.0	Joint Family	308	30.8
Other Specify	2	.2	Nuclear Family	629	62.9
n represent total participants			Living Alone	57	5.7
% represent per cent			Others Specify	6	0.6

In a social science research it is very vital to take note of the socio-demographic variables of the participants as it would impact on the results of the study. One variable may be responded with different options by the participants according to the level of understanding of the problem or their experience. The majority of the participants (46.3 %) were from the age group of 20-30 years, just above one fifth of the participants were from 30-40 years (21.2 %), just below one fifth of the participants were from >40 years (18.8 %) and least representation was found in age group less than 20 years (13.7 % of the participants).

Among the participants 58.6 % were male and 41.4 % were female, though author (researcher) could not make them equal half still, females were more enthusiastic to be the part of the study.

About 54.7 % of the participants were unmarried and 42.6 % of the participants were married. Altogether 2.7 % of the participants were divorced, widow and belong to other specify group mostly living away from their families.

The majority of the participants (69.1 %) were graduates, good number of participants (14.3 %) have attended secondary level of school education. Within the participants about 7.4 % have attend school until class 10, 4.8 % have attended ITI/Dip (industrial training) and 4.4 % have attend other courses such as IATA, short courses on welding, computers service and assembling, mobile repair and services, hair dressing and etc.

Incomes of the participants were realistic as figures show the minimum requirement to live in corporations of Tamil Nadu. Majority of the participants (42.2 %) had income less than Rs. 10000 (per month), 39.2 % of the participants had their income anything between Rs. 10000-20000. About 14.3 % of the participants had their income between Rs. 20000- 50000 while 4.3 % of the participants had their income more than Rs. 50000 per month.

The majority of the participants (62.9%) were living in the nuclear family system and 30.8% were from joint family system. About 5.7 % of the participants were living alone and 0.6 % was living away from the families.

Table 5.2: Participant's and their Father's Occupation

Options	n	%	Options	n	%
Participant' s occupation			**Father' s occupation**		
Student	362	36.2	Govt. employee	180	18.0
Private employee	215	21.5	Agrarian	143	14.3
Home maker	93	9.3	Business	129	12.9
Govt. employee	81	8.1	Daily wagers	129	12.9
Own Profession	70	7.0	Retired person	116	11.6
Daily wagers	53	5.3	Private employee	108	10.8
Retired person	41	4.1	Own Profession	102	10.2
Teacher/faculty	28	2.8	Home maker	20	2.0
Business	27	2.7	Teacher/faculty	15	1.5
Agrarian	13	1.3	**Other specify**	**58**	**5.8**
Other specify	**17**	**1.7**			

In a social research especially on corruption, it is worth considering the occupation of the individual's and their father's which shall account and share equal to relative knowledge of the issue. About one third of the participants were students (36.2 %), just more than one fifth were private employees (21.5 %), and about 45 % of the participants were from mixed groups including private and government employee, Home makers, professionals, daily wagers, retired personnel, teachers, businessmen and self employed, news paper merchant, etc., and being the agrarian (1.3 %). Father's occupation would greatly influence the views and emulate opinion on an issue, in real time father's occupation play a vital role in understanding corruption. Hence, this factor was collected for understanding the influence of the father's occupations in their opinion. The distribution of the father's occupation was very uneven and for majority of the participant's father's occupation was no way in connection with public sectors. About 80 % of the participants father were occupied as private employee, professionals, daily wagers, retired personnel, agrarian, businessmen, home makers and old goods agent, running hotels, self employed, news paper merchant, etc., and being the teachers (1.5 %). The profession, experience and practice are always hand in glow, but still, majority of the fathers were potential victim of corruption because they live in India. In the following chapter public ranking of the corrupt sector and scams are given, data are interpreted and discussed in detail with an inferential approach.

CHAPTER 6

PUBLIC RANKING OF THE CORRUPT PUBLIC SECTORS AND SCAMS

This chapter is exclusively dedicated for public ranking of the public sectors and scams including their experience and medium that influenced their ranking. Discussions are based on the inferential approach. Many of the researchers have theoretically concluded on several factors contributing to the act of corruption, in the discipline of criminological research this is the first empirical attempt to explain the corruption at grassroots. Transparency International (TI) conducted a survey in 64 countries with 50, 000 samples to assess public perceptions about corruption.

According to TI - The Global Corruption Barometer, the results were based and scored on 10 point scale (The Global Corruption Barometer, 2004), which is given in detail in the last chapter of this book. The results of the current research (main theme) are presented in form of tables, figures, the data interpretation and discussion/ deliberation are elaborated in simple terms to the level possible for better understanding and admiration of the results by the readers.

Public Ranking of the Public Sectors

To understand the public views on the public sectors it would be appropriate if public rank these government departments (public sectors) according to their choices with respect to corruption. **Annexure I** (Table A1) gives consolidated data and details on the rank in terms of numbers. Generally, in villages and small town public officers exercise more powers than any other. All the participants were able to rank at least top 5 corrupt departments but on the same event just 29.3 % of the participants were able to rate up to 10 public sectors. Rest of the participants completed their ranking of public sectors all 12. This is why author has decided to take up, top 5 five public sectors for discussion. While talking on corruption, media concentrated cases are trailed serious or at times cases involving public personalities. Hence, law becomes unnecessary and unenforceable in petty corruption cases.

In the Following Figures 6.1until 6.5 Abbreviation and Terms are as Follows

EB: Electricity Board

GPH: Government Public Hospitals/ Primary Health Center

Judiciary: Judges/Magistrate, Public Prosecutor, Defense Counsel and Courts

PDS: Public Distribution System (Ration Shops, Free Distribution Sarees, Dhotis, Televison

Sets, Mixer Grinders, Goats, Milchi Cow)

Police: Crime, Traffic, Law and Order

PWD: Public Works Department

Railways: Indian/Southern any other Zonal Operator of India

RD: Revenue Department (Corporation, Tehsil Office, BDO, Office of Revenue Inspectors)

RO: Register Office (Land/ Marriages/ Patta and Etc.)

RTO: Regional Transport Office

Trust: Trust/ Missionaries/ Welfare society/ NGO's

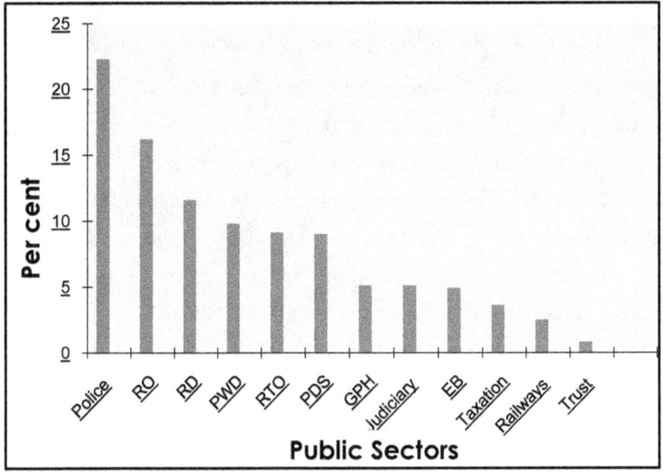

Figure 6.1.1: Public Ranking of the Public Sectors - First rank

Corruption and authority are two inseparable aspects of democracy, especially in city or town police have extraordinary authority over their jurisdiction. In general, when we ask anybody on matter of corruption, first comes the police, or any other agencies with which the individual have recent experience(s). To understand this, participants were given 12 public sectors for ranking the top corrupt public sectors shall be given number 1 rank. Among the public sectors, police (22.3 %) including crime, traffic, law and order where public contact are rare but still is ranked top corrupt public sector by the participants. Register office (16.2 %) and revenue department (11.6 %) were placed second and third, respectively, public work department (9.8 %) and regional transport office (9.1 %) were placed fourth and fifth top corrupt public sector by the participants. The trust (8 %) which includes four institutions was rated least by the participants.

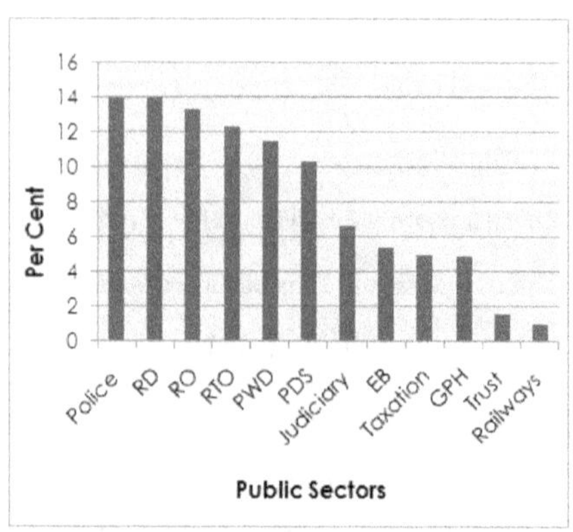

Figure 6.1.2: Public Ranking of the Public Sectors - Second Rank

The second choice should be close to that of first choice, is a normal social behaviour. In case of this study, it is very much evident; Corruption and authority are again ranked top in second top rank among given the public sectors by the participants, police (14 %) and revenue department (14 %) has been placed top in second most corrupt public sectors. Register office (13.3 %) and regional transport office (12.3 %) were placed third and fourth, respectively, public work department (11.5 %) was placed fifth top corrupt public sector by the participants. The railways were rated least by 1 % of the participants.

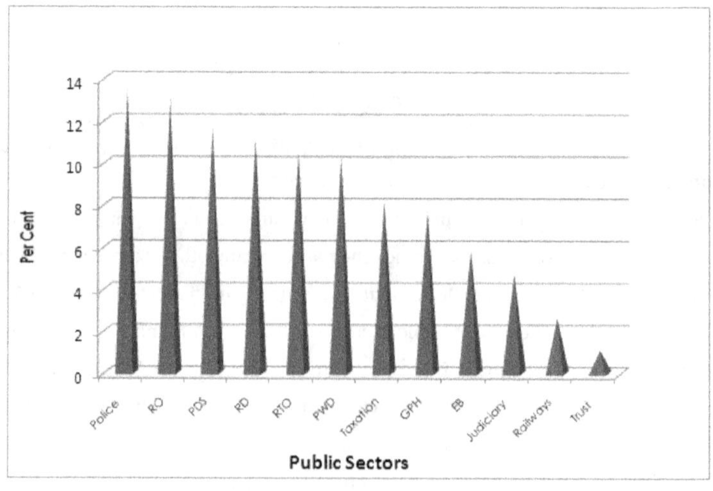

Figure 6.1.3: Public Ranking of the Public Sectors - Third Rank

From the figure 6.1.3 we can infer the details on the public sectors that have been ranked 3 by the participants. Again, police department has been given the apex place by 13.5 % of the participants, followed by the RO (13 %) and PDS (11.6 %) has been placed 2nd and 3rd, respectively. RD (11.1 %) and RTO (10.5 %) has been placed 4th and 5th rank, respectively. The least placed agency remains the Trust (1.1 %).

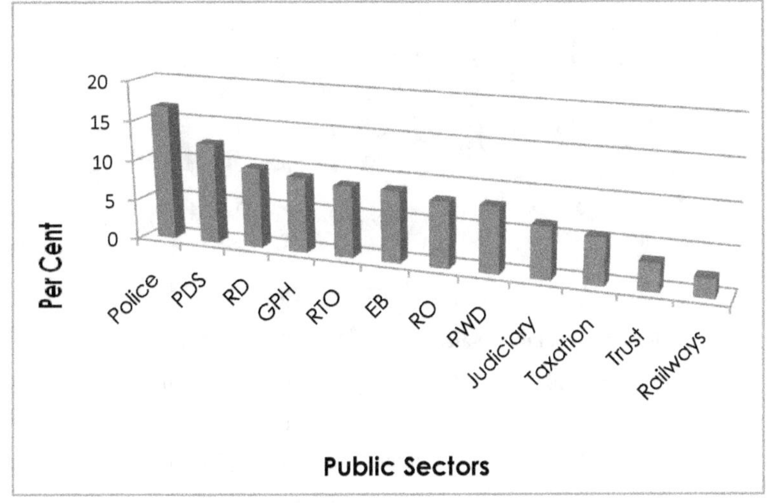

Figure 6.1.4: Public Ranking of the Public Sectors - Fourth Rank

The choice of the public will change or dilute when numbers increase is evident in the current study. From figure 6.1.4 it is evident that distribution of the public sectors has dispread. But, still top among the corrupt public sectors at 4th rank remains unchanged with police (16.7 %). PDS (12.5 %) has gained a position and move one step ahead, RD (9.9 %) at third place, GPH (9.3 %) join the top the row with 4th place, RTO and EB at the 5th place, by 8.8 % each of the participants. When we compare this response with the responses of rank 1, there is no change in 1st place, and all other positions have been replaced with some other public sectors. Once again participants have placed the railways as least corrupt public sector.

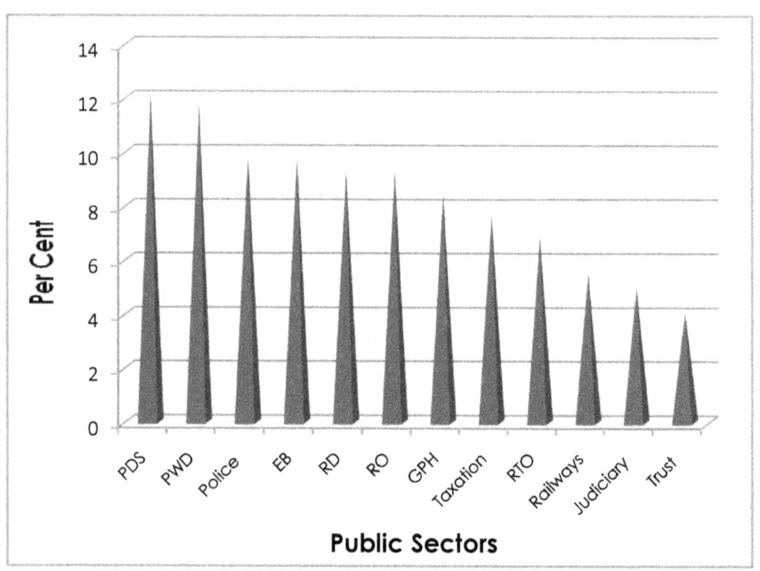

Figure 6.1.5: Public Ranking of the Public Sectors - Fifth Rank

Distribution of rank 5 is absolutely implausible; because all top 4 positions are occupied by the new public sectors, is evident from the figure 6.1.5. According to the participants PDS (12.2 %) has been placed at top followed by PWD (11.8 %), giving police (9.9 %) third place, EB (9.8 %) fourth place, RD and RO in fifth place by 9.3 % of the participants. Once again the least placed public sectors are Trusts, 4.1 % of the participants.

Table 6.2: Basis of the Public Raking of the Public Sectors and Influence of Media

Options	n	%	Options	n	%
Basis of the public rating			**Media influence**		
Personal opinion	494	49.4	Yes	521	52.1
Other experience	299	29.9	No	222	22.2
Media	207	20.7	Not Sure	257	25.7

From the above table we can infer that ranking of the public sectors by the participants (49.4 %) remains on their personal opinion, other half are duels of others sharing and media. The participants were confident to give their ranking based on given option; still it was necessary to understand in deep the influence of media on their option. For about 52.1% of the participant accepted that media has influenced them in giving the ranking to the public sectors.

Table 6.2.1 Participants Attention/ Interest on Corruption Matters

Options	Yes	No	Not sure
✧ Interested in reading the articles published in dailies	660	228	112
✧ Interested in reading the articles published in weeklies	448	405	147
✧ Follow news articles related to corruption on a regular basis	434	409	157
✧ Interested in listening to the news related to corruption in radio	370	499	131
✧ Interested in watching news relating to corruption in television	776	125	99
✧ Followed the articles on corruption published by Wiki leaks	291	524	185
✧ In your opinion do media play a prominent role in whistle blowing?	758	94	145
✧ Media cover only the corruption at higher levels of government?	550	236	214
✧ Media cover only the corruption at local levels of government?	353	327	320

The issue of corruption is routine in an individual life, only very few are not involved directly or worried, on the other hand many are worried or concerned and wanted to do something against this social milieu. Unfortunately many fail at very beginning of their fight, still hundreds of thousands of public wanted to do something against the officials involving in corruption, they do fail at the very first instance. In this regards, who can do anything and everything was only media. Media in recent past has influenced all the walks of life exercising its responsibility, appropriately. Hence, author felt it was necessary to understand the participant's interest on corruption with reference to the media, during the regular routine life. Majority of Indian have a primary effect of the media, if media report's news; it means something is wrong. In matters relating to corruption, participants (66 % and 44.8 %) agreed that they read corruption NEWS in dailies and weeklies respectively, and about 43.4 % of the participants, follow news related to corruption on a regular basis. As far as the electronic media is concerned it has some hype in it. About 37.6 % of the participants listen and 77.6 % watch news relating to corruption and 29.1 % of the participant followed the same in cyber world/space. Majority of the participants (75.8 %) were of opinion that media play a whistle blowing role in matters relating to corruption; just above half the participant (55 %) felt media only covers the corruption at high levels of the government or public sectors.

Table 6.3: Corruption- First thing that comes to Participants Minds

Options	n	%	Opinion was influenced	n	%
Politician	648	64.8	Media	648	64.8
Public (Government) sector	343	34.3	Personal experience	194	19.4
Private offices/ companies/ schools	9	0.9	Other experience	149	14.9
			Other Specify	9	0.9

Corruption is lobbying in our daily life, the participants were asked what comes to their minds when the term corruption is pronounced, for 64.8 % of the participants it was politician, 34.3 % it was public sectors and only 0.9 % felt of private offices/ companies/ schools. The ranking of politician (elected representatives) as most corrupt is evident from the results of the study conducted by the (CNN-IBN and CNBC-TV18, 2011). While it is choice of the participants, their opinion was influenced by the media for 64.8 % of the participants, 19.4 % on the personal experience and others experience was given by 14.9 % of the participants. It is necessary to note the media's role on the public opinion at large.

Abbreviation of Figure 6.4.1 Until 6.4.10

2G Scam: Distribution of 2G spectrum

IPL Scam: Indian Premier League

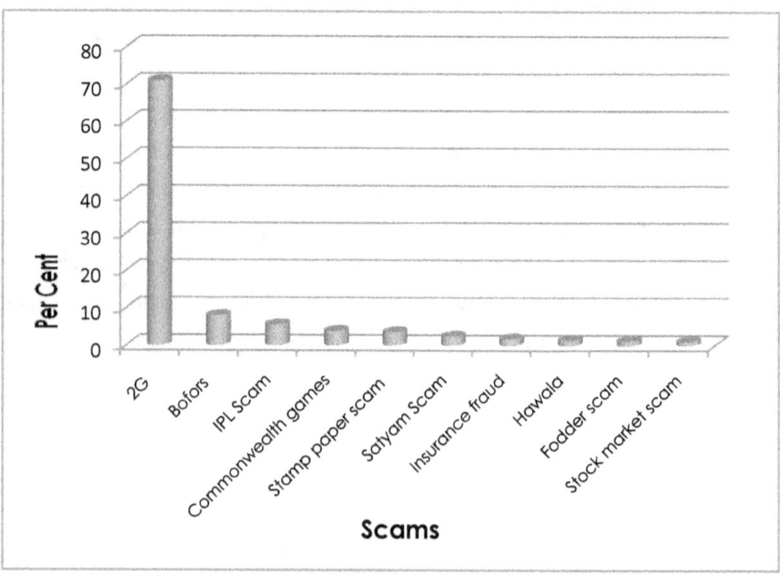

Figure 6.4.1: Top Scams and Public Ranking- First Rank

India is emerging as scam capital of the world since 1990's. So far, uncover scam show the complex nature of the corruption, people involved in, and how the actions are taken. The lethargy of the investigation and enforcement has slowly entered the corners of the judiciary making the judicial process more wariness. To check the public opinion on the scams, author has attempted to rank these scam by the participants. 2G scam was ranked the first by majority of the participants (70.9 %). Other options were not even ranked by the 10% of the participants. The consolidated data and total ranking in terms of number are available in **Annexure II.**

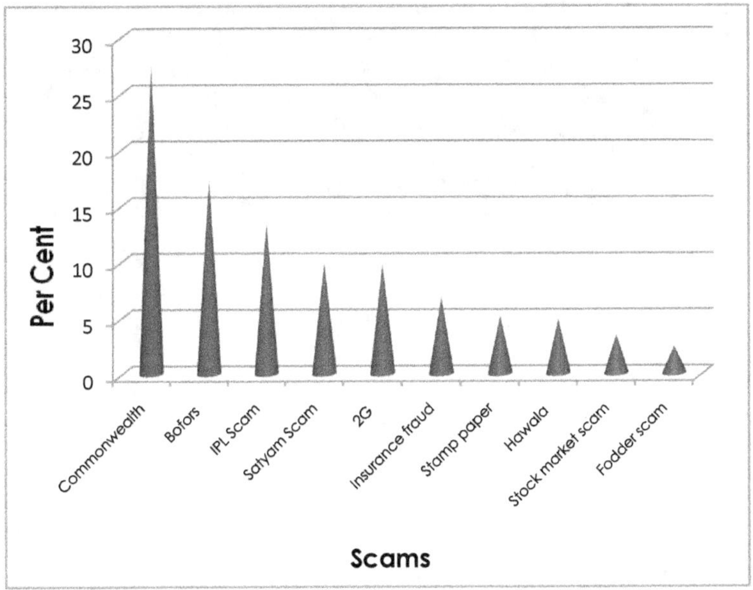

Figure 6.4.2: Top Scams and Public Ranking- Second Rank

Among the second rank scam, the top place was given to commonwealth game (27.4 %), 2nd was Bofors (173 %) and 3rd was IPL scam (13.3 %), as scored by the participants. It is worth to note that 2G scam was scored by less than 10% of the participants. Common Wealth Games scam involving then union sports ministry, Delhi chief minister and other involved were hyped by the media in order to show the seriousness of this scam. Bofors scam was one of the land mark corruption which turned the political history of the India, which involved not only defence matter but also, the public sentiments. India for more than a century is unable to find its position in sports because of corruption, way in and out are possible with corruption. It is

51

very rare to find sport arena of India without corruption. While small island nations are able to find a position in medal tally at Olympic Games, in India a gold medal is spoken several years or until the next Olympic. The important issue that affects the very spirit of the games in India is corruption, lack of appreciation and legal incentives attached to it. The recent IPL scam has damaged the spirit of the cricket in cricketing nation.

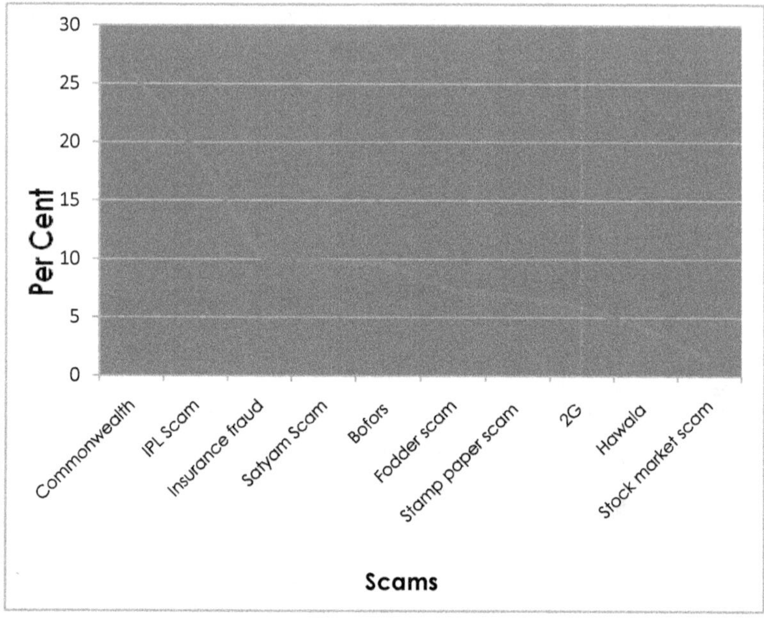

Figure 6.4.3: Top Scams and Public Ranking- Third rank

Again, majority of the participants scored the common wealth games (25.9 %) and seconded by the IPL scam (19.1 %). The new arrival to the list is Insurance fraud involving multi-national companies. Some millions of rupees are swindled through scams every year, the losers are none other the Indian citizens, who are share holders of leading companies alleged swindle.

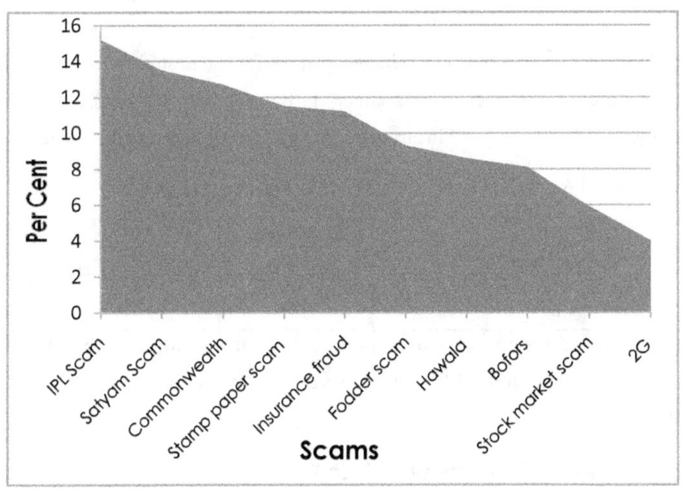

Figure 6.4.4: Top Scams and Public Ranking- Fourth Rank

Majority of the participants scored the IPL scam (15.2 %) and second was given to Satyam scam (11.5 %), third place was given to common wealth games by 12.7 % of the participants, stamp paper scam and insurance fraud were placed fourth and fifth places, respectively. The new arrival to the list is Insurance fraud involving multi-national companies.

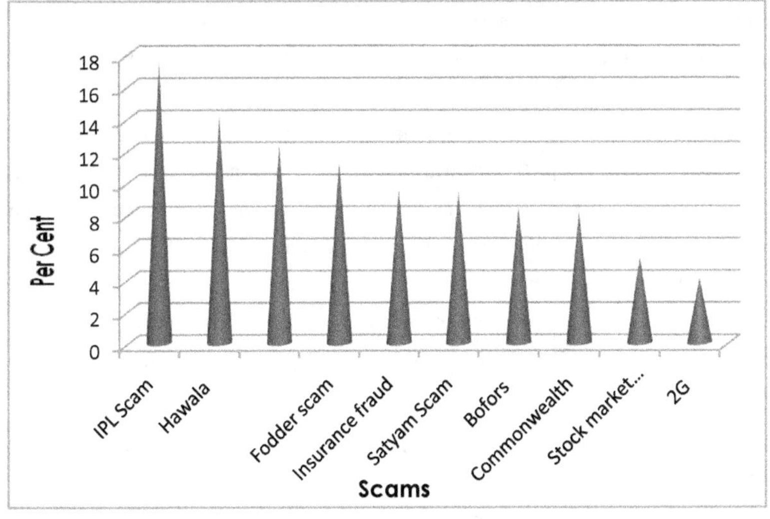

Figure 6.4.5: Top Scams and Public Ranking- Fifth Rank

Once again the choice of scams have changed except for the first place i.e. IPL scam by 17.6 % of the participants. Hierarchies of the scams were Hawala scam (14.1 %), stamp paper scam (12.3 %), fodder scam (11.3 %) and insurance fraud by (9.5 %) of the participants.

Table 6.5: Basis of Participants Rating of the Scams

Options	Frequency	Per cent
Personal opinion	118	11.8
Other experience	105	10.5
Media	777	77.7

Any ranking should have a basis, to majority of the participants (77.7 %) their responses were based on the media, about 11.8 % felt it was their personal opinion and 10.8 % learned it through others experience.

Deliberations on Top 5 Corrupt Public Sectors

Rank 1

It is common men belief that police is the most corrupt; police personnel are those with whom people come across daily but rarely have contact in their life; but this corrupt population can never be left unpaid because of their power of authority. In a similar study of this types police were one among top corrupt agencies with 3.6 points as given in the Global Corruption Barometer (2004). While in a study conducted by CNN-IBN and CNBC-TV18 (2011) police station was identified as most corrupt place by the respondents. In spite of several measures that are under serious purview to control corrupt, police are in enforcing positions which enable them to involve with no hesitations. It is too much to say other public sectors are bearable. Ravindra (2003 p 7) put forth that the common man is fast losing faith in the criminal justice system. It is not surprising why? A research study in the US identified cronyism as one of the factors responsible for the poor performance of the police force. The register office has been ranked second by the participant, after 1990's the public interest over procuring land for future has been established in the minds of the public at large. This has given a good hold to this office and higher chance of corruption by under valuing the land price and involve in corruption.

The office of the revenue department is flooded with crowd can be noted in any part of India, because of their authority over the public services, similar response was reported by CNN-IBN and CNBC-TV18 (2011) were Tehsil, BDO office was ranked as second most corrupt place. Register services was scored 3.0 points by the participants making it least among the mid level corrupt agency as given in the Global Corruption Barometer (2004).Why do public throng the gates of public offices is unclear because many times author has witnessed it, because of the dilatory procedures these office maintain over 5 decades. While too many cannot satisfy the requirement of them, unless and until approaches are clear about the formalities, procedures and practices in this office. It is surprising response from the participant ranking the PWD as fourth top corrupt public sectors. To this department public movement is rare still it has found its place. When taking in to account the RTO' s which do follow cumbersome procedures and practice, making public at large pay bribes in order to finish off their work. For instance they issue driving license to individuals who do not even recognize sign boards in roads, who do not indicate before they turn or know how to park a vehicle and many more.

The governments shall notify this office and find why there is so much of corruption in this public sector where hundreds of public move every day. The major problem is cumbersome and dilatory procedures; for, not too many of the literate public can fill the forms for the driving learner's licenses registered. Other important reasons are the documents issued by this office forms strong identification for further references, which is a birth right. For a common man Trust/ Missionaries/ Welfare society/ Ngo's are doing something to the poor and needy, at the same time it should be noted that funds generated and dealt by these agencies are huge. It is in this context that NGO's (civil society organisation in general) provide the global-audiences, constituency, think tanks are unable to be reach their goals, as many observers feel are still missing (Eigen, 2004 p 13). NGO's were one of the least corrupt agencies with 2.8 points as given in the Global Corruption Barometer (2004), in the same lines CNN-IBN and CNBC-TV18 (2011) recorded that NGO's and media as the least corrupt organisation.

Rank 2

Police has been ranked first with revenue department, is not surprising permit services (Revenue Department) was scored 3.0 points by the participants making it least among the mid level corrupt agency as given in the Global Corruption Barometer (2004). Third top being register office (RO), fourth being RTO and fifth being PWD is also not surprising. The least rated was railways, but according to the Central Vigilance Commission the most corrupt public sector in the country in terms of complaints received is railways. Public at large are unaware of the roles, duties and functions of the railways, hence it feeds a good image to the public. The number of corruption complaints received against the railways is increasing every year. According to the report of CVC railways have attracted more corruption complaints than any other government (public) sectors. The public opinion implies Indian railways are not transparent, its operation are secretly maintained and people have less frequent contact with this sector or of personal victimization or experiences.

Rank 3

This distribution show mere a slight modification in first place of the public sector, again police at top and RO at second place are acceptable, third comes PDS is little surprising because top 1 and 2 ranks it was not even placed in top five but it is now placed in 3rd position. This is surprising thanks to media, lot of cases on corruption in PDS has reached the public through them, also frequent report on the smuggling of the rice bags and distributing the freebies to party and family members of the ruling party, the participants opinion in this perspective is well influenced by media reports. In a similar study conducted by CNN-IBN and CNBC-TV18 (2011) ration shop was rated second least corrupt place. The smudging of the public sectors in the mind of the public is possible either by the personnel experience or through media. While public at large do not want to be corrupt but the rotten system require something to complete a work in the public sectors.

Rank 4

The choice and agencies are handy hence, public come up open to rank the public sectors with an easy appreciation. PDS has gained a position in public choice, it has been ranked second time in a row. This directly implies there is some mesh about the PDS; which has a less transparent, smudging procedures adding fuel to the fire, some of the goods are available in black market. One other agency that should be discussed is GPH which was never ranked before in top 5 places, the public hospitals are pathetic in condition in most of the city general hospital/ town's primary health center. Thiminappa (2003 p 11) inks there is a need to set up vigilance to check corruption in Government hospitals. Medical services were scored 3.3 points with customs by the participants, making them a mid level corrupt agency as given in the Global Corruption Barometer (2004).

In a similar study by CNN-IBN and CNBC-TV18 (2011) reported that government hospitals are least corrupt place. The public visiting these hospitals are not good enough to pay private medical practitioners otherwise nobody is interested in admitting or getting treatment with the government hospitals. Governments spend crores of rupees in building the facilities, medicine; appoint well paid physicians and etc., why still this agency comes to picture is a million dollar question! Many hospital and health centers are without proper facilities physician, nurses, toilets, medicine, ambulances, operation theaters, scan, medical laboratory facilities and so on, all because of corruption, it prevails at various levels from the peon until the chief physicians. No government employee is allowed to practice his profession outside their office and exceptionally physicians/doctors practice it as part- time in order to fill the financial gap or extend their service to needy in real-time. But after taking an appointment in government services with little gained experience, doctors work part-time in the parent institute and practice full time outside. Government is fully aware of this fact, still are unwilling to question these physicians in order to praise them and keep them in service.

Rank 5

Here, there is close ranking by the participants because of several reasons those department that were expected to be placed in top has been replaced. The new public sector that has to be concentrated is EB, though in Tamil Nadu, it is one least corrupt department for several years. Some recent unearthing of corruption inside this department; especially getting a new connection or three phases power supply after 2007 is difficult and it must have inched the public minds that EB is also corrupt sector. While CNN-IBN and CNBC-TV18 (2011) study reported that ration shops are second least corrupt place, this is only with reference to place i.e., ration shop and on the whole PDS at regional/area office are simply crowded with public where it takes months sometimes years for clearing the files or to settle the grievances of the public, some cases throng for months, corruption can make our work simple by only visiting the office twice or thrice.

Impact of Media on the Participants Ranking

The impact of media on responses is obvious, influence of father's occupation and family members experiences are also very much an influencing factor in ranking the public sectors, media remains the top choices in contemporary situations. Now a day's media is entrusted with higher responsibility in a democracy to carry the messages of the government and to portray ill functioning of the government. To this research media has played critical role of carrying the information of ill/mal functioning of the public system because, majority of participants had their knowledge of corruption through the media. It is high time that media reinstate ethics in them and train the new comers with strong morale, value and media ethics, so that in next few years we can see public fighting the rotten system with the support of media. In a study conducted by CNN-IBN and CNBC-TV18 (2011) it was reported that media as least corrupt organization, which is good to read on the other hands information on media corruption is also engulfing the media industry in India.

Deliberations on Public Attention/Interest in Corruption

Corruption at low level of the government or public sectors are very much important for discussion, but only 35.3 % of the participants felt media report these issues. Some important issues are taken seriously by the public at large, one such is corruption. Despite the fact that everybody feels they should fight it but the very rotten system demands and it replaces the pleasure of finishing work at shortest time. The media is stand-alone private body among the pillars of democracy, information's are assimilated to the public with commitment. Due to intense pressure of public, government of India has ordered for disclosure of details of the properties and savings of the public servants working with central government, its implementations are mostly at budding stage. However, some public servants have seen, read such orders while others have not seen orders. Venkatesan (2009) reports the public disclosure of assets by judges, though a welcome first step is certainly not the end, rather serious problem of judicial accountability or the lack of it.

Top Scams and Public Ranking

Rank 1

In recent years most spoken and heard scam in India should be 2G, since it involved the minister from Tamil Nadu it has really entered the minds of people in the state. The issue was reported in almost all news dailies for about 9 months from December, 2010 until August, 2011. While Dikshit (2010) calls it is a land mark year of scams, every section of the people in the state felt insult. In order to protect then Prime Minister's (Dr. Manmohan Singh) and other minister's involving top Minister and VIP's spoke on the issues for example Mr. MonteK Singh Aluwalia- the Vice chairman Planning Commission of India (The Hindu, 16 December, 2010 p 20) and Mr. K.G. Balakrishnan, former Chief Justice of India dimpled on the matter trying to exclude their choice of the ministers and VIP's (The Hindu, 08, August, 2010 p 12). If this is the interest shown to protect people of their choice what remains as social justice in this country?

Rank 2

Commonwealth games scam was lighted before the games took off; still the games continued everything went peacefully. This scam was charged against two responsible citizens, one Chief Minister of Delhi and other Mr. Suresh Kalmadi. Here again the supporters were equaled the expectation and matter went to deep pit. Dikshit (2010) comments play was off but fair justice was ???, one other Minister for Education, UT of Delhi- Mr. Lovely words it as No indictment of CM or Minister in CAG report (Lovely, 2011 p 10) as protecting statement.

Rank 3

Satyam scam was shocking information for its share holder in India, the share market impelled to foreign market which were safer compared to that of India. In India, general understanding of the public is that they do not involve in other than their area of interest henceforth when trouble emulates it damages good number of people in the country especially, when matter concerned with image of the entire country.

Rank 4

In the world there is no sport as cricket is played in India. The country is tagged cricket nation; any up and down in cricket will necessarily affect the country's cricket lovers. The first surprising scam involving the former Indian cricket captain Mr. Azharuddin, made people to hate cricket for little time, which was recovered by world's top batman's and bowlers of India. In order to repair the damages done a quick form of cricket with shorter time was introduced as 20-20 cricket. It reached every corner of India through Indian Premier League, which identified the cricket lover the young, energetic and smart player of the country. A scam involving match fixing, de tours, organization of the events all were tuned according to request of the bidders, it made a complete chaos in the cricketing system. One positive thing that was possible with other matters was immediate reaction was given to issue. Individuals responsible were removed form their designations. This event has jolted the Indian cricket fans; still Indians have selective amnesia, the very simple question, why and how it happened is un-answerable, the integrity of the individuals at responsible positions are absolutely unchecked *before their appointment.*

Rank 5

Hawala scam involving tax evasion by an individual amounting to rupees one lakh crores. The supreme court of India came up heavily on the government of India for not making any other cases to courts of India. It also, cautioned the enforcement for not being committed. Stamp paper scam involving 16 states, high government officials and former secretaries to the governments. Making a way the highest ever leak of the official stamp of India which went unchecked for more than 10 years. Fodder scam was another land mark corruption in India, involving animal, fodders and former Bihar chief minister. While fodders were purchased for livestock in record, really no livestock's were available under the state custody at that point of time. Finally, investigation revealed that no animals were maintained from the government during the period of purchase of fodders.

Participants Ranking and its Basis

In the contemporary India, the inter-personnel relationship have lost its value, it is media which plays a vital role in communication and exchange of information's. It may be television, cable, radio, internet, mobiles, telephone, or a social/public media. One thing is for sure that media carries the greatest duty of assimilating of the information to its users. Still some of the participants have opined on their personal experience and to some information was shared through their personal contacts. Though the research area was corporations still participants were maintaining some relations and shared their views. In years to come the participants experience will be influenced by sources such as internet or social media.

The major problem with corruption is that, it takes its own shape, size, color and encounters as observed by the individuals or group. Some detail data on the aspects of corruption is continued in the next chapter.

CHAPTER 7

PUBLIC ATTITUDE TOWARDS CORRUPTION, THEIR PARTICIPATION, VICTIMIZATION AND REPORTING BEHAVIOUR

In this chapter a full concentration of Part III data are presented, the data interpretation and discussion are given in simple terms for ascertaining the research outputs.

Table 7.1: Public Personalities and Corruption- Participants Opinion

Name of the personality	Corruption committed	Prevent corruption	Not Sure	How did you know			
				PO *	OC #	Media	
						Yes	%
Mr. Raja	873	10	117	6	97	808	80.8
Ms. KaniMozhi	824	7	169	3	83	793	79.3
Mr. Dayanithi Maran	659	19	322	3	76	740	74.0
Mr. Ramalinga Raju	506	40	454	4	87	639	63.9
Mr. Harshad Mehtha	465	62	473	4	77	626	62.6
Mr. Prasanth Bhusan	161	210	629	4	73	567	56.7
Ms. Kiran Bedi	116	475	409	6	83	650	65.0

* PO- Personal Opinion   # OC- Others Communication

In India, media play a vital role in dissemination of information especially on corruption. Media being the absolute source of corruption information, high end corruption involving public personalities are covered by them; over decade this is the scenario. The author wanted to understand participants' knowledge on public personalities and corruption. Hence, it was tested; ever column was filled by the participants. The public personalities in relation to corruption and anti-corruption in the recent past were given to the participants, among the choices, names of the alleged corruption committers and preventers were given. To majority of the participants (87.3 %) Mr. Raja (former union minister of telecommunication), Ms. Kanimozhi (82.4 %), Mr. Dayanithi Maran (65.9 %), Mr. Ramalinga Raju (50.6 %) and Mr. Harshad Mehta (46.5 %) have committed corruption. According to the participants the personalities such as Mr. Prasanth Bhusan (21 %) and Ms. Kiran Bedi (47.5 %) were rated corruption preventers. The opinion of the participants were mostly based on the media reports, the media information has influenced the responses anything between 80.8 and 56.7 % of the participants.

Table 7.2: Top Reasons of Corruption and Public Ranking

List of Reasons for Corruption	1	2	3	4	5	Total
Paid for an illegal work/entity to done	160	114	129	76	66	545
Don't like to spend much time in govt. offices	150	115	108	112	115	600
Urgent issue	136	112	133	129	108	618
Bribe demanding office setup	120	143	76	111	112	562
Individual laziness	112	120	134	77	153	596
Weak vigilance and anticorruption agency	89	62	110	120	79	460
Rotten system	82	96	82	77	87	424
Fearlessness of govt. staff towards the action against corruption	64	80	84	81	88	397
Do not know the formalities to complain	55	78	78	124	105	440
Low payment to govt. staff	18	22	26	22	38	126
Unaware of formalities	14	58	40	71	49	232

In order fight an issue it is mandate to understand the radical reasons. In this spirit, participants were given about 11 options to rate. The results came as shock, the top reason given by the participants (16 %, altogether 54.5 %) for corruption was given as paid for doing an illegal work/ entity, the second top response was did not want to spend time in government office (15 %, altogether 60 % of the participants), third place was given to urgent issue (13.6 %, altogether 61.8 % of the participants) which actually was scored high among all 5 ranks. Fourth and fifth response by the participants were bribe demanding office setup (12 %, altogether 56.2 % of the participants) and laziness (11.2 %, altogether 59.6 % of the participants), respectively. 8.9 % (altogether 46 %) of the participants felt it was due to weak vigilance and anti-corruption agency, 8.2 %, altogether 42.4 % of the participants responded that it is a rotten system, and for 5.5 %, altogether 44 % of the participants felt public are unaware of the formalities to complain on the corruption and related matters. The above data gives levelheaded idea on why public at large entertain corruption or become party to it. It is necessary at this point of time to understand the factors influencing their choices.

Table 7.3: Basis of Participants Rating

Options	n	%
Personal experience	421	42.1
Other experience	312	31.2
Media	267	26.7

Information from the table is very interesting and gives an important statistics, as 42.1 % of the participants ranking was based on their personal experience. About one third of the participants (31.2 %) opinion was based on the others experience. Media has impact 26.7 % of the participants.

Table 7.4: Participation in Corruption

Options	n	%	Options	n	%
Is bribing a crime			**Bribed for making work done**		
Yes	962	96.2	Yes	597	59.7
No	21	2.1	No	342	34.2
Not Sure	17	1.7	Not Sure	61	6.1
Was that a demand? (n=597)			**Was that for doing a legal thing/entity (n=597)**		
Yes	449	75.2	Yes	79	13.2
No	94	15.7	No	374	62.7
Not Sure	54	9.1	Not Sure	144	24.1
Interested in complaining the corruption cases			**Would like to be part of social bribing system**		
Yes	599	59.9	Yes	371	37.1
No	213	21.3	No	412	41.2
Not Sure	188	18.8	Not Sure	217	21.7
Support the corruption in public sector			**If yes, can corruption be decriminalize (163)**		
Yes	163	16.3	Yes	62	38.03
No	650	65.0	No	90	55.21
Not Sure	187	18.7	Not Sure	18	6.8

Public participation/ party to an act of corruption has become normal during course of life in any society especially in a democratic nation. For 96.2 % of the participants, bribing is a crime, about 59.7 % of the participants have bribed at one point of time to make their work done, 75. 2 % felt it was demand hence; they have to pay it, at the same time 13.2 % of the participants reported that it was for doing an illegal entity. 59.9 % of the participants were interested in complaining the corruption cases, 37.1 % of the participants were interested to be part of social bribing system while only 16.3 % of the participants support corruption in public sectors and among them only 38.03 % were interested in decriminalizing the act of corruption.

Table 7.5: Participants Experience and Corruption (n= 597)

Corruption Experience Was to achieve any of the following?	Yes	%	Not Sure
• For community certificate (birth rights)	334	55.9	25
• For getting driving license	327	54.7	15
• For income certificate	271	45.3	17
• For birth certificate (birth rights)	239	40.1	26
• For ration card (birth rights)	211	35.3	32
• For complaint the police station (birth rights)	201	33.6	30
• For death certificate (birth rights)	188	31.5	35
• For getting treatment in government hospitals (birth rights)	188	31.5	28
• For getting scholarship	131	21.9	40
• For TNGST/CST no	91	15.3	33

In India, there is possibility that any one at any time can be victimized by situation and become a party to corruption cycle. Even in matters that are called birth right one can accomplish only by paying the concerned public sectors, among the total participants, various issues/occasions for bribing was obtained. The above table gives the details of the issues, 55.9 % of the participants have paid to get a community certificate, which is a birth right of every citizen of India, driving license (54.7 %), income certificate (45.3 %), birth certificate- birth right (40.1 %), ration card- birth right (35.3 %), registering complain with police (33.6 %)- birth right, death certificate by a legal heir (31.5 %)- birth right, for getting treatment in government hospital- birth right(31.5 %), for getting a scholarship (21.9 %), and for issuance of TNGST/CST no (15.3 %). Lack of clarity of regulatory requirements and therefore applicable norms and the boundaries of acceptable behaviour is often seen as a typical feature of white-collar crime (Nelken, 1994; Zimring and Johnson, 2005).

Deliberations on Public Personalities and Corruption- Participants Opinion

In the contemporary India, the inter-personal relationship have lost its value, it is media that play a pivotal role in communications. It may be television, cable network, radio, internet, mobiles, telephone, or a Social/Public media. One thing is for sure, that media shoulder the greatest duty of assimilating the information to its users. Still some of the participants have opined on personal experience and some are in touch with the others so that information is exchanged. Though the study areas were corporations still there are exception areas in the entire corporation in order to maintain the relations and share shoulders. We can infer form the table 7.1 an information which is good source of data/knowledge to understand the nexus between the politician, corruption, public and media. The spate of corrupt public personalities as opined by the participants have given general idea that public at large are aware of some of the contemporary corruption that are unearthed and personalities connected with it, is a good sign that will benefit the future generations. These personalities have in recent past are very much popular and has extensive coverage in media. Especially, top respondent being Tamil was objective, as study was conducted in parts of Tamil Nadu participants could identify easily and share their views. In a study conducted by CNN-IBN and CNBC-TV 18 (2011) the order of corrupt are as follows Mr. A. Raja, Mr. Suresh Kalmadi, Ms. K. Kanimozhi and Mr. Dayanidhi Maran, the same is evident from the current research also, Since, Mr. Kalmadi was not given to the participants his place could not be confirmed. Incentives to engage in corruption are stronger when penalties for the abuse of power are weak and poorly implemented (Naunihal,

1998 p 194).

Top Reasons for Corruption

The reason given by majority of the participant show that any work with public sectors (government departments) could complete only with something paid for the work. Although tracing the history of corruption the reason for corruption was only to do some illegal work. Now the reasons for corruption stand elite with public servants need to be paid for doing their legitimate work. Forced and setup are two reasons for which every Indian should be worried and ashamed of, for doing a legitimate work public servants are targeting at sum, best example shall be the Register Office where anybody registering land should pay some percentage of value of the land. The third being fostering the work which show that public/government office don't compile with time factor, which should be taken seriously for consideration. The two reasons on which we shall be happy are reduce legal action and do some illegal work. However, the results of the research confirm that as Indian we are unable to realize our birth right in our home country.

Basis of Participants Rating

Here it is worth noting that media is not committed itself to fight this menace at large, though it publicize the matters of corruption it did not help in understanding the root causes/ reasons for corruption; especially at lower levels. It is sad that media unshielded their responsibility in giving information to its reader/beneficiaries on the methods to fight corruption.

Deliberations on Participant's Participation in a Corruption

According to the report of the Global Corruption Barometer (2004), whether the respondents have paid any bribe in last 12 month only 10 % of the participants agreed to have paid. This indicates a degree of disconnect: while those who admit bribing remain a relatively small percentage of all those surveyed, many of those surveyed express grave concern about petty and especially about the grand (Eigen, 2004 p 15). D' Souza, (2012 p 35) believes form of corruption that public life can encounter is the undermining of the system of government which has been given by the constitution. In a system named for lethargy and dilatory procedures make it possible, that anyone and everyone can be victimized at any time. There is more pathetic explanation given to corruption as demands claimed in order to pay to the superior officers. We are not sure how much is this information factual?

Deliberations on Participants Experience and Corruption

Democracy means informed citizens, in the world's largest democracy the situation is reverse. Anything and everything requires a sum, if it is connected with public sectors; in this regards it is good to convert our public system to private outsourcing. It is a shame in the world's largest democracy, to pay even for achieving a birth rights. Many factors have contributed to the shame of India; one thing that is indigestible is achieving birth rights, which is a complete violation of 2 each international and national instruments ICCPR and ICESCR, fundamental rights under the part III of constitution of India and the protection of Civil rights Act, 1997. Who can protect India if it goes this way? Achieving the status of super power will remain the dreams of the former president of India and many indigenous genius who wanted to see India foster in all the aspects of life. From the stand point of controlling corruption, focus on comprehensiveness may, thus, become counterproductive for several reasons (Naunihal, 1998 p 191). But, there are gaps in the policy and practice(s). In the next chapter we shall find information of the part IV data of the results, interpreted and discussed with basic inferential approach.

CHAPTER 8

OUTLOOK ON PUBLIC AWARENESS AND GOVERNMENT MEASURES TO CONTROL CORRUPTION

In a democratic country it is the primary duty of every government to make its citizens aware of what is happening in the country; that's why democracy means informed citizens. In the matters of social problems, government in centre or state, accord the intensity of problem on the basis of the rigorous impact on the society, and shall show interest to fight and keep the menace at bay. The serious preventive measures are attempted by government(s) to make aware the public at large on the issue(s). With reference to the corruption since government is party to it, it demonstrates lethargy and limited interest in promoting awareness, of late which is paralyzing the country's social security. In order to understand Hence, in this study author wished to the public awareness on the government measure to fight the issues of corruption.

Table 8.1: Participants Interest in Fighting Corruption

Options	n	%	Options	n	%
Fight corruption			**Corruption as a problem**		
Yes	635	63.5	Local	32	3.2
No	164	16.4	State	45	4.5
Not Sure	201	20.1	National	351	35.1
			International	572	57.2

Corruption is multi-faced issue hence, fighting shall start only with the individuals. There are more than dozens of laws, agencies, statutory or non-statutory organizations which alone can never fight the issues of corruption. The interests of participants (63.5 %) in fighting corruption were really appreciable. The fighting malaise of corruption requires not only the courage, passion more than that it demands patience with high tolerance. Though the participants are aware of the condition and contention of the corruption for majority of the participants (57.2 %) and 35.1 % of them felt the problem of corruption as an international in nature and national, respectively.

Table 8.2: Appreciating an Act of Corruption by the Participants

During our course of occupation	Yes	%	Not sure
• Favoring our neighbors amounts to corruption	696	69.6	100
• Favoring our relatives amounts to corruption	709	70.9	114
• Favoring our best friend amounts to corruption	662	66.2	125
• Using government properties such as using telephone for personnel use will amount to corruption	729	72.9	119
• Using government properties such as using Xerox copier for personnel use will amount to corruption	723	72.3	138
• Using government services such as telephone for personnel use will amount to corruption	698	69.8	155
• Using government properties such as computers for personnel use will amount to corruption	673	67.3	152
• Using government properties such as internet services for personnel use will amount to corruption	711	71.1	146

In recent times it is public attitude that they do not appreciate several deviant practices as deviance for examples smoking, drinking, dating, and corruption. In this sense author felt participants would not appreciate an act of corruption, it was surprising that majority of the participants in all the cases were able to recognize an act of corruption. Top appreciated act by the participants (72.9 %) was misappropriation of the public properties, on the other hands least appreciated act by the participants (66.2 %) was favoring our friend's amounts to an act of corruption.

Table 8.3: Reporting behaviour of the Participants and Reasons for Not-reporting

Options	Yes	No	Not sure
• Attempted to complain on the event of corruption	114	868	18
• Seen any officer being bribed	739	202	59
• Yes (n= 739) Made a complaint to the authorities	98	641	-
• Action taken against the complaint (n=98)	35	57	6
• Were you happy about the action (n=35)	13	19	3
• Rejection of complaint was informed (n=63)	7	55	1
Reason for not reporting the corruption (n=641)			
• No action will be taken	429	161	51
• Waste of time	397	207	37
• Problem in witnessing	295	306	40
• Fear of reverse action	292	310	39
• Unwillingness	290	290	60
• No faith in police	280	308	53
• Don't know whom to report	266	336	39
• Fear/shame	263	308	70
• Fear of police	261	338	42
• Police will act on their own	111	450	80

Reporting an act of crime is the duty of every citizen; many in the world's largest democracy are unwilling, why? In general participants were asked about history of complaining an event of corruption, only 11.4 % of the participants have attempted. Majority of the participants (73.9 %) have seen an officer being bribed, only 9.8 % have a made a complaint, among these complaints only 35 cases were taken action, only 13 participants were happy about the action taken and in case of rejection of the complaint 7 cases were informed of the reasons for not taking action.

Table 8.4: Participant's Awareness- Government Measures and RTI

Options	Yes	%	Not sure
• Aware of department of the vigilance and anti corruption (V and AC)?	728	72.8	42
• Aware of the contact address of the office of the V and AC	190	19.0	62
• Aware of the phone numbers of the office of the V and AC?	150	15.0	68
• Aware of the prevention of the corruption act?	343	34.3	102
• Does it deal with corruption in public services? **(n=343)**	101	29.5	119
The Right to Information (RTI) Act, 2005			
• Aware of the Right to information (RTI) act, 2005?	397	39.7	4
• The right to information act was enacted to ……? (n=397)			
• To achieve our birth rights.	217	54.7	69
• To fix accountability and ensure transparency in government working	322	81.1	36
• T o eliminate corruption and bribe in public bodies.	238	59.9	71
• Ever used RTI? (n=397)	90	22.3	-
• Was the attempt a successful one? (n=90)	47	52.2	16
• Yes, was it a successful attempt (n=47) i. Personal interest and satisfaction	14	32.5	7
ii. Public cause	23	53.5	2
iii. Benefit of others	24	55.8	6

From the above table 8.4 we can infer that about 72.8 % of the participants are aware of the office of Directorate of Vigilance and Anti Corruption. It is good to note that people living in corporations are aware of this department. About 190 participants were aware of the location/ address of office of Directorate of Vigilance and Anti Corruption. Among the participants 150 participants had contact number of the same office. An act/law fighting corruption introduced in the year 1947 and replaced with amendments in the year 1988 was known to 34.3 % of the participants and only 10.1 % are aware of the role of the act. Here, the quote of the Indian Penal Code is questionable "Ignorantia juris non excusat"- **Ignorance of Law- No excuse**. In theories explaining corporate crime, state responsibility was reduced to a lack of state regulation or a lack of enforcement (Box, 1983 p 64) or, going back to Sutherland, was conceived as belonging to the same social class (Sutherland,1961 p 248).

Table 8.5: Awareness of RTI among the Participants and their Experience

Options	n	%	Options	n	%
Knowledge of the RTI act, 2005(n=397)			success story of winning issues through RTI (n= 397)		
Personnel experience	30	7.6	Yes	259	65.3
Others shared	157	39.5	**Source of knowledge on success stories (n=259)**		
Media	210	52.9	Personal experience	22	8.5
			Other experience	157	60.6
			Media	80	30.9

Any thing human knows come of external learning, the participants knowledge of RTI was induced by the media to 52.9 % of the participants, others shared their knowledge was scored by 39.5 % of the participants and 7.6 % learned of their own. Participants who have knowledge/experience of success stories of winning issues through RTI were 259 cases. The source of success stories came from others experience to 157 cases, to 80 participants media have portrayed and 22 participants have learned through personal experiences. There is no other ways of ensuring transparency and accountability, but the Right to Information. It is the key to authentic, effective and clean governance and vibrant democracy. (Kalshian, 2004 p 7), in an argument sense it is important that private sectors should also be governed under the RTI act, Anand (2011 p 6) felt private companies should be ready to face a law like RTI. After a decade, RTI remains unthreaten to corrupt because of its unclear administration with no permanent high commandant. Hence, the objectives of this act are again tested and influence of polity weakens tentacles to implement the premiere public friendly legislation.

Table 8.6: Knowledge of Lok Pal and Jan Lok Pal Bill

Options	n	%	Options	n	%
Aware of Lok Pal Bill			**Aware of Jan Lok Pal Bill**		
Yes	587	58.7	Yes	460	46.0
No	295	29.5	No	401	40.1
Not Sure	118	11.8	Not Sure	139	13.9
Lok Pal Empowered with	Yes	Not sure	**JanLokPal Empowered with**	Yes	Not sure
• Punishing politician	467	53	• Punishing politician	389	33
• To control all forms of corruption	413	82	• To control all forms of corruption	385	47
• Punish all corrupt	401	70	• Punish all corrupt	372	40
• Punish public servant-central government	380	88	• Punish public servant- central government	345	59
• To control corruption at higher level	372	93	• To control corruption at higher level	343	66
• Punish public servant- • state government	390	90	• Punish public servant- • state government	339	58
• To control corruption • lower (grassroots) level	355	101	• To control corruption lower (grassroots) level	338	57
• Increase power of the investigation agency's	299	117	• Increase power of the investigation agency's	331	55

The latest arch in fighting the corruption, by the government of India is trying to enact LokPal act through a bill, for which high power committee was formed with Mr. Anna Hazare as chairperson, which was declared dispersed on 09 August, 2012 in an interview by the chairperson. About 58.7 % of the participants are aware of the LokPal bill and 46 % of the participants are aware of the Jan LokPal bill. While these bills are yet to be finalized still participants ranging between 299 and 467 were able recognize the aims and objectives of these bills. LokPal bill is well thought-out (Sen, 2012 p 32). Then Prime Minister of India commented Lokpal will help, but will not solve the problem of corruption (Singh, 2011). He also continued saying that there is no single solution to a problem and there was a need to act at multiple fronts. The complaint on the task is not adequately appreciated. In the contemporary world corruption is a part of social orders (Karat, 2015 p 14).

Some Relevant Appreciation with Deliberations

As far as, the reforms to be implemented, will be an overload on government that scarce public resources and attention would be spread thin. India's experience with corruption has shown that laws, rules, regulations, procedures and methods of transaction of government and business sounds excellent however cannot by themselves ensure effective and transparent administration. Mechanism to observe, prevent, monitor, and punish corruption are not adequate nor have they proved to be effective to the extent that they exist. For dealing with the overwhelming problem of corruption the best position for civil society is in a coalition consisting of 3 pillars: government, the private sectors and civil society (Naunihal, 1998 p 188). Recognizing the perils of corruption, nations are trying to create effectives anti-corruption measures for both the public and privates sectors (Editors, 2004 p1).

Deliberations on Participants Interest in Fighting Corruption

Among the responses something that was unbearable was corruption was recognized as local including regional and district was given by 3.2 % of the participants. It was a national problem for 35.1 % of the participants. While many of us are interested in fighting corruption still, it lacks clarity in approach and to individuals with their own life style makes it impossible to fight the system of his/her own. Hence, we shall join some organizations that really struggle against corruption. In a statement Bhushan (2012) commented that civil society should take part in policy making to fight corruption.

Deliberations on Appreciating an Act of Corruption

From the table 8.2 we can infer that public at large (at least 2/3) could definitely differentiate an act of corruption from a common act. In this context, the doctrine of criminal law i.e., the Indian Penal Code *"Ignorance of Law- No excuse"* is not justifiable. In the globalized world knowing that we are doing something against the law is very common, people around us comment on that as pessimistic behaviour. Hence, recognizing the act of corruption is not enough, to commit is individuals' choice.

Deliberations on Reporting behaviour of the Participants

If you find bribery or corruption, then come boldly but when I say boldly, because of coming to complain except you be very sure to prove the justice of your cause (Naunihal, 1998 p 103). It is imperative to note that 59.7 % of the participants have bribed hence, their opinion in this circumstance shall considered as vital reasons for not reporting. The top reason for not reporting an act corruption is no action will be taken (42.9% of the participants), 39.7 % among the participants felt it was waste of time, 29.5 % records problem in witnessing, 29.2 % expressed fear of reverse action, 29 % of the participants were unwilling. To some handy participants no faith in police (28 %), not sure of whom to complaint was felt by 26.6 %, 26.3 % added fear/shame, 26.1 % had fear of police and to 11.1 % police will act on their own.

Deliberations on Participant's Awareness- Government Measures and RTI

The latest instrument to fight corruption is Right to Information Act (RTI) which provides public ample access to the information of the public sectors records and many other documents which MLA or MP can access. It is sad to note that public living in urban/ corporations are unaware of such tools. Only 39.7 % of the participants living urban Tamil Nadu are aware of the Right to Information Act, 2005. Among the participants between 217 and 322 were able to respond on what the act deals with. Only 90 participants have used RTI and 47 succeeded. 43 participants failed, which was used on public causes (23 cases), benefits of others (24 cases) and out of personal interest and satisfaction (14 cases). In this regard the onus is spate of media, according to the words of former Chief Justice of India, vigilant press is vital to fight corruption and injustice (Balakrishnan, 2010 p 12).

Suggestion/Mechanisms for Effective Combat of Corruption in India

For instances the greatest issue in implementation of the laws fighting corruption is Government (s) have never studied social impact analysis of any law in force while efficacy of legislation should conduct researches on regular intervals.

- Stop allowing any social bribing; declare all the government institution as corruption free zone, as in practice the spit free zone.
- Zero tolerance should be maintained in all the state.
- Every state should study corruption in their jurisdiction continuously and assess the situation and act accordingly. In this process students of the discipline of Criminology and Criminal Justice may prove worth, by way of research as they are aware of corruption its causes, consequences, and methods to control or suggest suitable measures through their research.
- Government should be transparent. In India, The Right to Information Act, 2005 has "already engendered mass movements in the country that is bringing the lethargic, often corrupt bureaucracy to its knees and changing power equations completely.
- Training people on Right to Information Act, 2005 at large scale starting from Panchayat members to Ministers, shall be the first step in countering the corruption.
- Dedicate a branch of vigilant officer with no criminal record or corruption charges and extract report from their respective offices in their working ministries.

Polity

In India the most hated professional by an intellectual is politics. There is no mechanism to control or measure their activity, it is therefore a considered the most uncomfortable position to be held by gentlemen's. Though there are rules prohibiting a person to contest election with a FIR booked but in practice nothing is stoppable.

- Any individual booked under First Information Report (FIR) shall be suspended temporarily or removed from the position of MP/MLA/ Ministers.
- When FIR is booked do not allow candidates contesting in MP / MLA election, although the law prohibits those individuals, this law is toothless without serious practices. The election commission of India needs to take necessary action promptly.
- Codify special bill to maintain on the asset of the elected Member of Parliament and legislative assembly.

- Confiscate all the property of the corrupt, in case of public servant (including politicians), family members shall be made ineligible for appointment to any government employment.
- Political parties should check corruption in their respective parties because political corruption can be controlled.
- Limit the public participation in government. Any individual should be allowed to be MLA/MP only for maximum of 2 terms in their lifetime, in this regard constitution of India shall be amended, which is the need of the hour.
- If any elected member is proved for an act of corruption, he may be suspended or removed from the post at the earliest.
- Government should notify the corrupt in their respectively ministry through their official website, which shall deter the corrupt.

Enforcement Agency (s)

- Police are mostly attached with corruption to many of the agencies especially media; if the situation remains the same; policing may be private as in territory of California, USA. Otherwise what is the use of having a police system which is against the public at large? This failure is basically connected to lack of control by the intelligence and vigilance agencies in India. In a study Umarhathab (2007) found that regional transport office ranked number one among the most corrupt department. Media reports corruption in rarest of the rare cases, not too many public has witnessed the arrest of the public servant in front of the public or vigilance officer coming on a surprise check on vigilance.
- Office of vigilance requires some quality and action oriented officer which means these officer should be recruited exclusively rather work on a deputation expect for the higher post, at all other level recruit should be exemplary for example students of Criminology/ Police Science-Studies/ Criminal Justice, who are inculcated with the knowledge of crime, law, investigation and social welfare are better choice.
- Strengthen the office of Vigilance and Anti-corruption in terms of numbers, as existing strength is inappropriate and certainty of action is impossible.
- To win the public confidence, it is necessary that police should work against the corruption in public place.

- A special recruit of officers considering students of Social Science especially from the discipline of Criminology and Criminal Justice with special interest on Vigilance and Anti-corruption department may contribute to the existing counter efforts.
- Enforcement is entrusted with detection and investigation but should be elaborated on the cases with research.
- Academic research output and think tanks should be recognized through annual conferences exclusively for officer working with Anti-Corruption and Vigilance department.
- Policy recommendations of researches should be well taken and put in action before loses its validity.
- Enhance the staff strength in vigilance and anti-corruption agencies in accordance with the recommendation of international agencies.

Judiciary

- Speed up the trail as well set up a time limit for each case at rate of 3 months for non-cognizable and 6 months for cognizable offences. While in corruption cases maximum time limit should be restricted only to 6 months.
- CVC should involve in portraying birded in internet and also use other communication media to establish corrupt and charges against them.
- Whistle blower should be protected; this shall increase reporting of any incidence of corruption.
- Whistle blowers should be rewarded or awarded medal in commemoration for their service to corruption free India.
- Exclusively court should be set for dealing with corruption cases at district level.
- An association/ committee/ society/ forum shall be formed in order to enable judiciary answerable, this shall avoid or, perhaps reduce the disparities in judgments, especially in corruption cases.
- The above committee should recommend for amendments/ draft act required act or up grade the existing law according to requirement or changing situation on regular basis (every 6 months).
- Official of the Criminal Justice shall be trained in duty conscious and social responsibility, this is one way of enriching their commitment during their service and after.
- Criminal Justice Department (s) should be made autonomy with accountability.

- Establish separate court to deal with certain section of people, especially the corrupt and to forfeit their properties.
- Criminal justice official shall be trained as tech savvy in order understand the public view and opinion through interaction in social media, which is inevitable in days to come as people go unfair towards the justice.
- Unwanted formalities may be removed in order to reduce unnecessary delay during trail.
- Punishment for corruption cases shall be made appropriate, severe and certain.
- Amend the PCA allowing for restraining the family members of corrupt to enter public services including polity for at least 2 generations.
- Lastly, punish the convicts who involve in corruption more than a time with depriving of civil rights and except for basic human rights. Also, socially restrain the family member of the corrupt and shall be put under scanner.

Transparency International is a global organization that seeks to empower civil society to participate in efforts to fight corruption. Here are some ways advocated (and implemented) by this nonprofit organization with which India can make a difference: To make system workable and fight the threats it is good to organize the following matter and act according to the recommendation of the

(i) Public debate on contemporary issues in combating corruption

(ii) Transparency in government

(iii) Protecting the whistle blower

(iv) From an integrity circle

(v) Remove temptations of the contemporary corruptions in the country and finally

(vi) A macro level research at state or district level to understand the situation on regular interval.

To a greater extent the policies and practices have not changed the situation of corruption in India, but one step is hoped at combating corruption through access to information(s). Again the responsibility of popularizing the act/law is left with the government(s) and however, it does not show any interest over the matters of combat mechanism witness the nexus between corruption and polity. In the following chapter an elaborate discussion on the prevention techniques is detailed.

CHAPTER 9

CORRUPTION, LAW AND PREVENTIVE MEASURES

Corruption is a serious problem eroded in to Indian administration; it is widespread, deeply rooted, well-organized and tolerated. Which is un-stoppable in an instance/stretch; the basic input of corruption is inaccessibility of information. In order to prevent such matters law allows the public to approach and access the information. With reference to corruption India as an independent country is in more trouble than in any others hand. After the introduction of the concept of globalization, situation has worsened, is evident from the recent revealing of the scams. This is the season of scams and the biggest ever corruption cases in India have been unearthed more recently. So, we decided to dig deep to see which scams were the biggest and most damaging to the country and its citizens alike. These scams are heavy weight in nature which influences individuals until the state policy; according to Top Scams in India (2010).

Top 10 Scams of India

1. 2G Spectrum Scam

We have had a number of scams in India; but none bigger than the scam involving the process of allocating unified access service licenses. At the heart of this alleged Rs.1.76-lakh crore worth of scam by a former Telecom minister of India? Who according to the CAG, has evaded norms at every level as he carried out the dubious 2G license awards in 2008 at a throw-away price this came to light only in the year 2010, the very significant milieu was by the time 3G spectrum was auctioned.

2. Commonwealth Games Scam

Another feather in the cap of Indian scandal list is Commonwealth Games involving Mr. Suresh Kalmadi. Even before the long awaited sporting bonanza could see the day of light, the grand event was soaked in the allegations of corruption. It is estimated that out of Rs. 70000 crore spent on the games, only half of the said amount was spent on Indian sportspersons. The Central Vigilance Commission, involved in probing the alleged corruption in various Commonwealth Games-related projects, has found discrepancies in tenders – like payment to non-existent, wilful delays in execution of contracts, over-inflated price and bungling in purchase of equipment through tendering – and misappropriation of funds.

3. *Telgi Scam*

Each and every scam must have something unique in it, to make money out of it in an unscrupulous manner- and Telgi scam had all the suspense and drama that the scandal needed to thrive and be busted.

Alleged Mr. Abdul Karim Telgi had mastered the art of forgery in printing duplicate stamp papers and sold them to banks and other institutions. The tentacles of the fake stamp and stamp paper case had penetrated 12 states and was estimated at a whooping Rs. 20000 crore plus. Mr. Telgi clearly had a lot of support from government departments that were responsible for the production and sale of high security stamps.

4. *Satyam Scam*

The scam at Satyam Computer Services is something that has shatter the peace and tranquility of Indian investors and shareholder community beyond repair. Satyam is the biggest fraud in the corporate history to the tune of Rs. 14000 crores in India. The company's disgraced former chairman kept everyone in the dark for a decade by fudging the books of accounts for several years inflating revenues and profit figures of Satyam.

5. *Bofors Scam*

The Bofors scandal is known as the hallmark of Indian corruption. The Bofors scam was a major corruption scandal in India in the 1980' s; when then Prime Minister Mr. Rajiv Gandhi and several others including a powerful NRI family named the Hindujas, were accused of receiving kickbacks from Bofors AB for winning a bid to supply India's 155 mm field howitzer. Most of all, the Bofors scam had a strong emotional appeal because it was a scam related to the defense services and India's security interests.

6. *The Fodder Scam*

In this corruption scandal worth Rs.900 crore, an unholy nexus was traced involved in fabrication of "vast herds of fictitious livestock" for which fodder, medicine and animal husbandry equipment was supposedly procured.

7. *The Hawala Scandal*

The Hawala case to the tune of \$18 million bribery scandal, which came in the open in 1996, involved payments allegedly received by country's leading politicians through hawala brokers. Thus, for the first time in Indian politics, it gave a feeling of open loot all around the public, involving all the major political players being accused of having accepted bribes.

8. *IPL Scam*

The list of scandals in India is just not ending and becoming grave by every decade. Most of us are aware of the recent scam in IPL and embezzlement with respect to bidding for various franchisees. The scandal already claimed the portfolios of two big-wigs in the form of Mr. Shashi Tharoor and former IPL chief Mr. Lalit Modi.

9. *Insurance Fraud*

Although not corruption scams, these have affected many people. There is no way that the investor community could forget the unfortunate Rs. 4000 crore Mr. Harshad Mehta.

10. *Stock Market Scam*

Wherein over Rs. 1000 crore Mr. Ketan Parekh which eroded the shareholders wealth in form of big market jolts.

All these scams are basically out of non transparent approach but, the access to information through the law made it possible to sweep these scams which are of Himalayan heights. Hence, access to information is boon to the democracy. In the last part of this chapter an exclusive deliberation on the access to information is detailed. While prevention of corruption is possible with strong legislations and enforcement, this challenge is never beaten by the existing anti-corruption system of the world's largest democracy. Whether law is capable of doing a minute change in the scenario is another question, with no answer for several years.

Legislations Dealing with Corruption and Anti-corruption

Since, corruption is mostly economic in nature, it is necessary to look at laws dealing with economic crimes in India. Majority of the economic crime laws does not cover corruption directly rather the fringes of act of corruption are well seen in these laws. For instance below given are laws that deal with economic offences in India.

Table 9.1: List of Laws Dealing with Economic Offences

S. No	Economic crimes	Acts / Legislation
1	Tax evasion	Income Tax Act
2	Illicit trafficking in contraband goods (smuggling)	Customs Act 1962 & COFEPOSA, 1974
3	Evasion of Excise Duty	Central Excise Act, 1944
4	Cultural object's theft	Antiquity and Art Treasures Act, 1972
5	Money laundering	Foreign Exchange Regulations Act, 1973; Money Laundering Act, 2002
6	Foreign contribution manipulations	Foreign Contribution (Regulation) Act, 1976
7	Land grabbing / Real estate frauds	Indian Penal Code
8	Trade in human body parts	Transplantation of Human Organs Act, 1994
9	Illicit drug trafficking	Narcotic Drugs and Psychotropic Substances Act 1985 & NDPS Act, 1988
10	Fraudulent bankruptcy	Banking Regulation Act, 1949
11	Bank frauds Insurance Frauds	Indian Penal Code
12	Racketeering in employment	Indian Penal Code
13	Illegal foreign trade	Import & Export (Control) Act 1947
14	Racketeering in false travel Documents	Passport Act, 1920/ Indian Penal Code
15	Credit cards fraud	Indian Penal Code & IT, 2000
16	Terrorist activities	Indian Penal Code & POTA
17	Illicit trafficking in arms	Arms Act,1959
18	Illicit trafficking in explosives	Explosives Act, 1884 &Explosive Substances Act, 1908
19	Theft of intellectual property	Copyright Act, 1957(Amendments 1984 & 1994)
20	Computer/software crime piracy	Copyright Act, 1957 / IT Act, 2000
21	Stock market manipulations	Indian Penal Code
22	Company frauds	Companies Act, 1956 / Indian Penal Code, MRTP Act, 1968

Other vital laws that can be used against the act of corruption includes

- Delhi Police Establishment Act 1946

- Inquiry Act 1952

- The Benami Transactions (Prohibition) Act, 1988

- The Prevention of Money Laundering Act, 2002

- Central Vigilance Commission Act 2003 and

- The Lokpal and Lokayuktas Bill, 2013 is Act No. 1 of 2014.

Response to Corruption- Prevention

Do We Live in a Democratic Country?

India's experience with corruption has shown that laws, rules, regulations, procedures and methods of transaction of government and business of administration excel but cannot by themselves ensure effective and transparent administration. It is midst of the time were corruption is a social order. Naunihal (1998 p 188) observes mechanism to prevent, monitor, and punish corruption are not adequate nor have they proved to be effective to the extent that they exist. It is in this context that NGO's (civil society in general) provide the global audience, the global constituency, the global think tanks that many observers feel is still missing (Eigen, 2004 p 13), in India the need of hours is an agency that is serious and dedicated to fight corruption, here we need to appoint Mr./Ms. Clean. For dealing with the overwhelming problem of corruption the best position for civil society is in a coalition consisting of 3 pillars: government, the private sectors and civil society. If the reforms are implemented it is an overload on government that scarce public resources and attention would be spread thin. From the stand point of controlling corruption, focus on comprehensiveness may, thus, become counterproductive for several reasons (Naunihal, 1998 p 191). Recognizing the perils of corruption, nations are trying to create effective anti-corruption measures for both the public and privates sectors (Editors, 2004 p1).

Agencies Fighting Corruption

Even before independence of India, the British had established the Delhi Special Police Establishment (DSPE) to control corruption which surged during the Second World War. The prevention of Corruption was enacted in the year 1947, and Administrative Vigilance Division (AVD) was created in home ministry in 1955. In each ministry Vigilance officers are appointed or depute to enquire in to charges of corruption in their respective ministries.

The Central Government, in order to fight corrupt practices that are prevalent in various Departments, PSUs, Nationalized Banks, Insurance Companies, Autonomous Organizations and other similar bodies, has established the following organizations :

(i)   Central Bureau of Investigation

(ii)   Central Vigilance Commission

(iii)   Administrative Vigilance Division in the Department of Personnel and Training

(iv)   Vigilance Units in Ministries/Departments and their Subordinate Offices

(v)   State Vigilance and Anti-Corruption agencies/ bureaus and

(vi)   Lokayukta- subject to interest of state government.

The above agencies of Government of India or state government are responsible in their own way for eradication of corruption in their areas of authority. Apart from the Central Bureau of Investigation, none of the four agencies are empowered to register criminal cases against corrupt public servant, and take up the investigation. They have greater role in taking preventive measures with a view to achieve a corruption free system in various government departments. In case the suspect public servant commits any misconduct by violating the rules and regulations of the department concerned, their acts of misconduct are enquired into and punitive actions as specified in the respective conduct or service rules. In this regard, all the vigilance and anti-corruption officials of various organizations are expected to work in close association. Right from the first step, i.e., collection of intelligence with reference to corrupt activities of tainted public servants, conducting joint surprise checks in the stores, public sectors and government organisation etc. providing documents for inspection during secret verification, necessary assistance at the time of investigation, including processing the request for sanction for prosecution, assistance during Regular departmental action (RDA) proceedings etc.,

The superintendent of police of CBI meets the CVOs of various departments in order to exchange necessary information with the departments concerned. This meeting is generally known as coordination meeting during which decisions to conduct joint surprise checks, finalization of (i) agreed list of suspected officials, (ii) list of officers of doubtful integrity, (iii) list of points and places of corruption, (iv) list of undesirable contact men are decided. Besides, pending cases of the branch, documents relating to verification of Complaints/FIRs, pending sanction for prosecution, pending matters concerning suspension/transfer of tainted public servants, old and new RDA matters, are also discussed? We are unable to understand even after so many steps we still maintain a pathetic situation and why conditions remain unchanged?

At times it is seen that the final order of the disciplinary authority is communicated to the concerned branch of CBI for commenting on adequacy of the punishment. The CVO do not have the powers to take action against the suspect officials, for their criminal misconduct, such matters may be forwarded to the CBI. The CBI after registration of a FIR against a public servant- invariably sends a copy of FIR to the concerned vigilance department for their information and necessary action. During the course of investigation also, assistance of the Vigilance Department is required for various reasons, including summoning of witnesses, seizure of documents/articles, the logistic support, like, availability of accommodation, vehicle, witnesses for search/arrest etc. In case of arrest of accused person, the information with regard to the arrest of the accused public servant is sent to the concerned vigilance department for taking necessary suitable action.

Prevention of Corruption Act, 1988

To deal with corruption amongst public servants in India, the existing laws are amended (Prevention of Corruption Act 1988) or new law will be enacted, replacing the Prevention of Corruption Act, 1947. PCA 1988 incorporates provisions of chapter IX of the Indian Penal Code to deal with Public servants and those who abet them by way of criminal misconduct and enables attachment of their ill gotten wealth obtained through corrupt means. This act also widens the scope of definition of Public servants. Public servant means any person in the service, pay of the government, or remunerated by the government by fees or commission for the performance of any public duty. Public duty means a duty in the discharge of which the state, the public, or the community at large has an interest. The 'State' includes a corporation established by or under a central, provincial or state act or an authority or a body owned or controlled or aided by the government or a government company defined in section 617 of the Company's Act 1956. In India, in addition to a large number of health and educational institutions, the government also aids many other kinds of organizations. Hence, the employees of such bodies are also covered by this act.

Corruption and Legal Framework

Few sections of the statutory law (IPC) of India, discuss on the illegal gratification and corruption. Still, in the year 1947 an exclusive law was enacted to prevent the act of corruption in public life and service; which was amended as *"The Prevention of Corruption Act, 1988" (PCA)*.

According to Sec. 13(1)-(D) PCA, 1988

Investigation of Case Relating to Abuse of Official Position The ingredients of the offence of criminal misconduct as defined under Sec. 13(1)(d) of Prevention of Corruption Act, 1988 reads as under :-

Sec. 13(1)(d)

A public servant is said to commit the offence of criminal misconduct, If he:
i.   *by corrupt or illegal means, obtains for himself or for any other person any valuable thing or pecuniary advantage; or*
ii. *by abusing his position as a public servant, obtains for himself or for any other person any valuable thing or pecuniary advantage; or*

iii.   while holding office as a public servant obtains for any person any valuable thing or pecuniary advantage without any public interest." Thus, it would appear that Sec. 13(1)(d) is divided into three parts, viz., 13(1)(d)(i), 13(1)(d)(ii) and 13(1)(d)(iii) and each of these three is distinct offence.

The common ingredient for all these three set of offences is accused committed an offence of criminal misconduct as a public servant and he obtains any valuable thing or pecuniary advantage for himself or any other person. Whereas for the offence 13(1)(d)(i) is committed by adopting corrupt or illegal means, 13(1)(d)(ii) through the abuse of official position and 13(1)(d)(iii) on the grounds of without any public interest. In order to establish the charges under section 13(1)(d) of the Prevention of Corruption Act, 1988, the IO has, therefore, to collect evidences on the following counts, besides proving that at the time of commission of offence the accused was a public servant as defined u/s 2(c) of the Act :

a.   Accused committed an offence of criminal misconduct as a public servant.

b.   Obtained any valuable thing or pecuniary advantage either for himself or for any other person.

c.   Means adopted for commission of crime were either corrupt or illegal or as a result of abuse of his official position or the receipt of valuable thing or pecuniary advantage obtained for any person were without any public interest. Here, the word "abuse" has to be distinguished from the word "use" and "misuse". Mere misuse of authority as a public servant does not attract Section 13(1)(d)(ii) of the P.C. Act.

The word 'abuse' is a transition from the word 'use'. It is a third stage in matter of intensity and culpability. The second stage being 'misuse' (use + violation) of rules, procedures or any aberration from the established norms. For 'misuse' to become 'abuse' another factor, namely, mens-rea is a must, which in turn implies dishonesty. To prove dishonesty wrongful gain or wrongful loss and mens-rea (wicked intention) has to be proved. In IPC, 'dishonestly', wrongful gain and wrongful loss have been defined which read as under:

"Dishonestly": Whoever does anything **with the intention** of causing wrongful gain to one person or wrongful loss to another person is said to do that thing "dishonestly".

"Wrongful gain": "Wrongful gain" is gained by unlawful means of property to which the person gaining is not legally entitled.

"Wrongful loss": "Wrongful Loss" is the loss by unlawful means of property to which the person losing it is legally entitled.

The details of points to be looked into during course of investigation of a case of abuse of official position are summarized below:

(i)   *Award of Contracts*

a.   Not issuing proper notice inviting tenders and inviting them from only chosen parties.

b.   Disclosing the offers of others to the chosen party.

c.   Not choosing the lowest tendered for invalid reasons.

d.   Approving a tender which does not conform to specifications when other such tenders are available.

e.   Accepting a tender after the time limit.

f.   Giving the order to a person who has quoted high or who is in the black list or whose performance in the past has been repeatedly poor.

(ii)   *Execution of Works*

a.   Allowing escalation when there is no justification.

b.   Allowing use of substandard material.

c.   Allowing substandard construction.

d.   Allowing deviation from approved plan.

e.   Allowing extension of time when there is no justification.

f.   Providing departmental material or labour when the contract does not specify the same.

g.   Allowing removal of material supplied departmentally.

h.   False measurements (of earthwork etc.) and paying more to the contractor.

(i) Allowing additional final payment without justification.

Note: In (f) and (g) above Criminal Breach of Trust may also be attracted.

(iii)   *Purchase of Material*

a.   Not inviting tenders and placing the orders on a favored party.

b.   In spite of tenders, placing order on a higher tendered for no valid reason.

c.   Approving and accepting substandard material.

d.   Accepting less than the actual quantum to be supplied.

(iv)   Other Miscellaneous Acts

a.   In assessment/refund orders by Income Tax Officers, Sales Tax Officers, Excise Officers etc.

b.   By Customs officials by imposing (i) no duty (ii) less duty (iii) assistance in smuggling etc.

c.   Bogus Muster Rolls, manufacturing records, transportation records etc.

d.   Gross misuse of technical manpower, tools, equipment's and machineries by an unauthorized providing to the contractor free of cost, when it is not provided in the contract.

Investigation of Cases

Investigation of cases relating to abuse of official position is difficult in nature. Generally, investigation of these cases should be centered towards collection of evidence, both oral and documentary, keeping in view the ingredients of Sec. 13(1) (d) of the Prevention of Corruption Act, 1988. The seized documents should be got proved by oral evidence, if possible and the circumstances so warrant, the opinion of the expert should also be obtained on various aspects of the case to pinpoint the identity of the accused as well as his omissions and commission. Normally, the investigating officer should collect the following documents and examine witnesses:

(i)   Documents to be Collected

a.   Papers relating to the posting of the public servant.

b.   Papers relating to the duties and responsibilities of the public servant.

c.   Papers relating to the financial delegation of powers of the public servant.

d.   Papers relating to the procedures etc. in the office.

e.   Relevant files relating to contract or purchase etc.

f.   Personal file (including property return) etc. of the public servant.

g.   Rules relating to contract, purchases etc.

h.   Documents of the favored party (by conducting a search, if necessary).

i.   Documents with the public servant.

   For this purpose, if necessary, his residence, office and bank lockers will have to be searched on the strength of search warrants and certified copies of bank accounts and relevant original pay-in-slips and cheques of the public servants as well as the favored party to be obtained.

j.   Other relevant documents.

(ii) ***Witnesses to be Examined***

a. Concerned officials of the department to prove the rules, procedures, financial delegation of powers, personal files of public servant, relevant files relating to the contract, purchase etc.

b. Employees of the favored party.

c. Experts to prove the mode of execution of the contract (substandard construction, substandard supply of materials, supply of material beyond specification etc.).

d. Bank officials to prove the bank transactions.

e. Other relevant witnesses.

During course of investigation, attempts should be made to collect documentary and oral evidences against the public servant as well as the private party to prove their willful nexus and criminal misconduct of the public servant. Attempts should also be made to collect evidence to establish the aspect of pecuniary advantage obtained by the public servant. After conclusion of investigation and receipt of the final orders of the competent authority, the SP's report should be sent to the competent authority for obtaining sanction for prosecution u/s 19 of the P.C. Act, 1988. On receipt of the sanction for prosecution, the investigating officer should prepare a charge sheet for its submission to the competent court.

The PCA, 1947 has in built provisions for delay, prolonged litigations and evasion while the act of 1988, is meant to fight with existing weak justice system. Menon, (2011) writes why should there be one set of rules for the centre and another for the states in dealing with corruption? While centre seems to be stern in dealing with corrupt politicians, many states seems to be soft- peddling the issue. Law is always encountered whenever development is high in relation to that of crimes in a country but for, Eigen (2004 p 13) dysfunctional legal system may be the cause in one country; the transition from a hierarchical, traditional rural society to today's global village may be the principal cause, elsewhere. Which was expressed by Shailendra, (2011 p 24) we do not need more laws to curb corruption but more truthfulness. The journey towards more honest and transparent society is a long way and will require making the powerful horns and honest more powerful.

Access to Public Information

The access to public information is very much necessary to fight the corruption at lower level of the government was prioritized and several countries introduced exclusive legislations especially by the Europeans countries, even before 200 years. Those countries after 2 centuries have been rated and are maintaining the top position in corruption free countries. The introduction of an act in order to access the public information was termed in different manner, the aim and the objectives of the law/act are almost the same. The Right to Information(RTI)/ Freedom of Information (FOI) act is the same. This act/law was introduced by 67 countries prior to India. However, India is appreciated for the enacting the world's best piece FOI as "RTI" Act, 2005.

Table 9.2: Hierarchy of the Introduction FOI/RTI Law/Act

S. No.	Country	Year
1.	Sweden	1766
2.	Colombia	1888
3.	Finland	1951
4.	U.S.A	1966
5.	Denmark and Norway	1970
6.	France	1978
7.	Australia and New Zealand	1982
8.	Canada	1983
68.	India	2005

All of sudden government of India ascended to enact the Right to Information Act. It was successfully enacted and introduced as RTI Act, 2005. The main objection of the act is enlisted below with explanations.

Why Right To Information Act?

It was intended to make realize the following to citizens of India.

- To achieve our birth rights.
- To fix accountability
- To ensure transparency and
- To eliminate corruption and bribe in public bodies/sectors.

What is Right to Information Act, 2005?

Every citizen of India has the right to get information within a period of 30 days from

- Government Departments;
- Government Undertakings;
- Government Aided Organizations
- Any private body in which Government or other agencies having access to information including government /government aided/ PSU/ autonomous agencies/ sectors.

What is Information?

Information means any material in any form including records, documents, memos, e-mails, opinions, advices, press releases, circulars, orders, logbooks, contracts, reports, papers, samples, models, data material held in any electronic form and information relating to any private body which can be accessed by a public authority under any other law for the time being in force -Section 2(f), RTI Act, 2005.

What are the Information's we can Access/ Get/ Check?

Every citizen shall have the right to obtain any information which can be accessed by MLA or MP. Any citizen of India shall

- Inspect records,
- Inspect samples,
- Inspect site and working place,
- Obtain copy of note files; current files and photo copies (ammonia copy) of even ancient records of more than 20 years from the alone cited public sectors.

While government counter measures against corruption is aimed at successful concealment of the act, still in real time it is never so. In the forthcoming chapter the role of private sector in fighting corruption is elaborated and concluded.

CHAPTER 10

ROLE OF PRIVATE SECTORS IN FIGHTING CORRUPTION

Anti-corruption efforts in India have largely been focusing on the public sector which is called the "demand side" in the parlance of corruption economics. The private sector which forms the "supply side", which actually pays the bribes, has been largely ignored. The supply side theories often put the onus of fighting corruption on the private sector. It states that firms pay bribes primarily for overcoming their shortcomings in terms of - poor quality of their product/service, high price of their product or to create a market for their goods which otherwise are not in demand. Thus they pay bribe to stay in competition despite these handicaps or to avoid true and fair competition. Corruption under globalization is the anti-thesis of a free, fair, competitive and efficient society, as it distorts the objectivity, transparency and fair play in the Indian societies. Though it has not been a successful attempt for 3 decades, one thing that can create some good, honest, and committed citizens is that moral education. The Indian educational system evaluate only the knowledge of sciences, arts, history, commerce, management or economic and etc., but never the morale, value and ethics of the individuals. Hence, it is high time to debate on role of private agencies in fighting corruption.

The Role of Private Sectors/Agencies in Corrective Measure

To address the challenges in fighting corruption, India needs to integrate anti-corruption measures in all spheres, collect the responses of all walks of life, induces financial crisis and climate/environment/office ambience and change to commitments as recommended by the international community, which will eradicate poverty and enhance social equality. For this reason Transparency International (TI)-India advocates earliest ratification and stricter implementation of the UN Convention against Corruption (UNCAC), the only global initiative that provides a framework for putting an end to corruption.

TI's Corruption Perception Index is based upon corruption-related data from 13 source surveys published, from 10 independent and reputable institutions in the world whose studies are well documented and the methodology published to enable an assessment of their reliability. For instance CPI (2010) was calculated using data from 10 out of 13 surveys (excluding ADB, AFDB, and Economic intelligence Unit) has been used for India. The subjects, the source, and the points (out of 10) given by the institutions for India are summed and final score of out of 10 is given to India.

- *Government's capacity to punish and contain corruption – **Bertelsmann Foundation***
- *Transparency, accountability, and corruption in Public Sector – **World Bank & IBRD***
- *Extent of corruption as practiced in governments, as perceived by the public and as reported in the media, as well as the Implementation of anticorruption initiatives – **Freedom House Foundation***
- *Likelihood of encouraging corrupt officials, ranging from petty bureaucratic corruption to grand political corruption – **Global Insight***
- *Institutional Framework – State efficiency: 'Bribing and corruption exist/do not exist' – **IMD International, Switzerland,** World Competitiveness Centre*

-All above – IMD World Competitiveness Yearbook

- *How serious do you consider the problem of corruption to be in the public sector – **Political & Economic Risk Consultancy (PERC)***

-As above – Asian Intelligence Newsletter

- *Undocumented extra payments or bribes connected with (1) export and imports, (2) public utilities, (3) tax collection), public contracts, and (5) judicial decisions are common/never occur – **World Economic Forum (WEF)***
- ***Global Competitiveness Report (2010).***

Some of the Transparency International- India's Initiatives

According to the Annual Report (2008 p 5 and 6) of this organisation it has been actively engaged in the campaign/journey against corruption, together with other like-minded civil society organizations like Lok Sewak Sangh, Gandhian Satyagraha Brigade, FACT-India, MKSS, Parivartan, Public Affairs Centre, Campaign for Judicial Accountability and Reforms, Citizens' Forum Against Corruption, Association for Democratic Reforms, Lok Satta, 5th Pillar of India, India Against Corruption, Act India etc. It has been pursuing, *inter alia*, for

- The passage of the Lok Pal Bill
- The Corrupt Public Servants (Forfeiture of Property) Bill
- Ratification of the UNCAC and transfer of funds lying in secret bank accounts abroad
- Integrity Pact (IP) that has been adopted by only 39 out of 200 public sector undertakings and the Ministry of Defense (none of the public sector undertakings of the States has adopted the IP)
- Notification of the rules under the Benami Transaction (Prohibition) Act, 1988
- Lokayukta(s) in all states with adequate powers for taking action against the corrupt
- Strengthening of the Central Vigilance Commission

- Passage of the Judicial Standards and Accountability Bill for transparency in judiciary
- Electoral reforms to prevent those charge-sheeted for heinous offences from contesting electoral office
- Police reforms as per the decision of the Supreme Court of India in *Prakash Singh* judgment
- Strengthening of the prevention of Corruption Act and removal of the restriction (Single Directive) that requires sanction of the competent authority even to initiate an enquiry into charges of corruption against senior officer of the rank of Joint Secretary or its equivalent
- Independent Central Bureau of Investigation
- Training of officers in integrity
- Citizens' charters with penalty clause in all pubic departments
- Social audit
- Ethical standards to be observed by the corporate sector and
- Role of the Planning Commission in monitoring the expenditure of money, grants, subsidies, and laying stress on outcomes rather than outputs (statistical formality), etc.

However, the political establishment in India is showing little interest in addressing the above counter measures. It is sure if these measures are taken seriously and taken to their logical conclusion, there would be an improvement in India's standing in the world community (Bawa, 2010). All the corrective measures undertaken against corruptions are striving hard to end the menace. One large area of concentration which is always left untouched is understanding public opinion, experiences, their participation and check the reach of anti-corruption activities of the government of India and states. Why these attempts have failed at large or has not contributed to better the situations in India, there are innumerable threats in the world's largest democracy, which are left unnoticed hence, any progress is impossible. The threats includes

i. Tradition of Integrity (The report Santhanam Committee, 1964; Hanlon and Pettifor, 2000; Neild, 2002; Chopra, 2009; Umarhathab, 2011).

ii. Absence of Autonomy and Accountability of Criminal Justice Official and their Social Responsibility (Umarhathab, 2011).

iii. Slow Motion Justice (Menon, 2009) -*Appeal, Revisions, Writs and Review*

iv. Disparities in Verdict, Judgment, and Sentencing (Umarhathab, 2011).

v. Lack of Agency(s) (Umarhathab, 2011) to control the government offices

vi.   Lack of use of Technology and Scientific Approach (Gupta, 2001)

vii.   Lack of Policy Researches, Awareness and Transparency (Hanlon and Pettifor, 2000; Neild, 2002; Chopra, 2009; Sreevatsan, 2009; Umarhathab, 2011).

There are information's on the successful efforts to counter corruption by most corrupt of the countries in the world but never in India. There are models emulated of experience by some of the nations. Bhattacharya (2007) elucidate Indonesia, perceived as one of the world's most corrupt country, anti-corruption measures proved to be surprising effective. A newly constituted anti-corruption commission and the adhoc (temporary) courts put the governor of Aceh Province behind the bars for 10 years for his role in multi-million dollars bribery scandal, this will never happen in the world's largest democracy. It would be better for India to emulate Chinese in order to rid the country of corruption. The strictest punishment should be meted out to those who comprise the nation's polity, economy and security for money. Sengupta (2003) opines more public involvement, not more legislature is required to receive the slackening fight against corruption. Hong Kong Model is another successful model, still we do not know how far it can help the Indian situations. The anti-corruption strategy involved investigation, prevention, education and enlistment of support, simultaneously. Hence, the result was in favor of the anti-corruption efforts by the government of Hong Kong.

Understanding corruption is important for several reasons. Corruption has infiltrated into all aspects of public life making people lose their faith in democratic institutions because of a perilous mix of bureaucracy, corrupt politicians and criminals in a hybrid, potent and poisonous witch's brew. Corruption has been blamed for the failures of certain "developing" countries to develop, and few empirical researches have confirmed a link between higher perceived corruption and lower investment and growth (Mauro, 1995; World Bank, 1997). At the same time, corruption is viewed as one of the main obstacles that post-communist countries face in attempting to consolidate democratic institutions and open market economies (Shleifer, 1997). Yet very little is known conclusively about what causes corruption to be higher in one place than another. The figures of the enforcement agency are unrealistic and do not show any real time picture, an attempt has been made to understand the position of corruption at grassroots (Mid-low level public sector).

There are enormous issues which have spider the crime of corruption. The research has successfully achieved the objectives of the study and results have shown an unfavorable condition that prevails in the contemporary Indian Administrative System. The research has given rudiments of the public participation and their reasons for the involvement also; it has given us the knowledge on the lack of government's efforts to popularize the anti-corruption measures. Participants at large are willing to fight corruption but they are unaware of what to do? How to do? Whom to approach? Whether a reverse action is possible? What lacks with public offices. Hence, this attempt to research corruption at grassroots has raised several unanswerable questions, and has lighted issues pertaining to available system and public sentiments at large. Hope, the research undertaken has chalked out the gaps in procedures, practices and the policy, at the mid and low levels of the public sectors.

Epilogue

Corruption is aged as society, which has rooted from the beginning; on the other hand it is unrealistic to expect a corruption free country. Corruption is not confined only to the phenomenon that are discussed in the earlier chapters, but much depends upon the environment, procedures and practices of the public sectors, many time it includes the personal character/morale of the individuals in the administration and that of the members of the public. It is however clear, that unless concrete action is taken, the level of corruption will only increase. What are required to curb corruption are both the reform of the public sectors and a change in attitude by the private sectors (NCAS, 2004 p 23). There is growing culture that corruption is inevitable because it is experienced from birth to death in India. Human behaviour is also deemed to be governed by the circumstances and the social environment. There is a much better grasp today, of the extent to which corruption is a symptom of fundamental institution weaknesses and is witness from the results of the study. Naunihal (1998 p 191) wrote focus shall be on the need to redesign and improve the underlying framework of our basic public institution that serves all sector, their structures and system in order to achieve corruption control.

There are fundamental problems in our process of evaluation, eligibility, recruitment and training, because the recruitment of the public officials, the team of recruits looks only at capacity of the individual to handle the issues at any cost is actually the failure of the employer because the employees will always try to impress on the employers with his/ her behaviour moral, ethical, attitude, standards or even without any of the above, depending on the employer. Naunihal (1998 p 191) argues that improved recruitment, career development and reward systems in the civil services will go a long way in institutionalizing a more efficient and responsive bureaucracy that will be less corruption prone. One form of corruption which will remain unbeaten in closed societies of India is nepotism (favoritism); it has greased the Indian society for more than 6 decades. At the national level, India still does not have an ombudsman type, LokPal legislation and machinery to deal with corruption among ministers and higher bureaucracy (Naunihal, 1998 p 188), it is good time that government of India and states shall concentrate on the implementation of the laws rather try new laws; also try to implement the recommendations of the National Police Commission (1977-81), for instance, improve the morale and accountability of the police who are responsible for enforcing laws including those pertinent to corruption control, systematic reforms of the laws, regulations and institutions.

Public at large should love to go police station the current situation is vice-versa. In order to make it possible to fight corruption, the task of fighting shall be outsourced to non-profit and professional organization such as transparency international or autonomous organisation such as Directorate of Vigilance and Anticorruption or Central Bureau of Investigation with special recruits. Any government agency established with a mission to fight corruption shall be used only if they are autonomy and accountable, which will help to achieve its mission. To cite few measures that are felt by other researchers to combat corruption are, Naunihal (1998 p 192) recommends four essential action areas for building a national agenda for corruption control:

a) *Reforms of the political process,*

b) *Restructuring and reorientation the government machinery,*

c) *Empowerment of citizens and*

d) *Creating sustained public pressure for change.*

It is not uncommon to anti-corruption efforts at the micro-level being subverted by the corrupt political leaders at higher levels (p 193). The author has suggested ways and means to fight/combat corruption in India in the chapter VIII after exclusive working in this area for a deceda. According to Transparency International that seeks to empower civil society to participate in efforts to fight corruption, here are some ways advocated (and implemented) by this nonprofit organization with which can make a difference:

- *Demand transparency*

- *Be a whistle blower and protect them*

- *Form an integrity circle to fight the issues connected and*

- *Continuous public debate and implementing law with zero tolerance*

As a statement of conclusion, the measure and prevention strategies suggested in this work would reduce the corruption to an extent. However, this may help policy makers, enforcers and executives of laws to extend their course of action, to say that corruption will totally disappear if these measures and prevention strategies are successfully implemented is to say too much, on a theoretical ground, still situations may improve.

References

- Abey, K. (22-28 Nov, 2010). Decoding 2G scam. India Currents, (pp. 27- 29).

- Ali. A.M and Crain W.M. (Winter 2002). Institutional Distortions, Economic Freedom, and Growth. Cato Journal, 21(3), (p. 416).

- Anand, U. (July 2011). Companies should be ready to face a law like RTI. Civil Society, 8 (9), (p. 6).

- Annual Report (2008). Transparency International-India. Retrieved 24 July, 2012 from http://www.transparencyindia.org/resource/annual-report/Annual%20 Report%202008.pdf

- Balakrishnan, K.G. (December 18, 2010). Vigilant Press Vital to Contain Corruption and Injustice. The Hindu (News daily). (p. 12).

- Balasubramaniam, A.V., (July, 2011). People's Union for Civil Liberties, 8 (9), (p. 6).

- Bauman, Z. (1999). Globalization: The Human Consequences. U.K., Cambridge: Polity.

- Bawa, P. S. (October 26, 2010). India – Continues to be Corrupt- Press release, New Delhi.

- Bayley, D. H. (1966). The Effects of Corruption in a Developing Nation. The Western Political Quarterly, 19(4), (pp. 719-732).

- Bhattacharya, A. (7 Jun, 2007). For the Love of Money. The Telegraph, (p. 4).

- Bhusan, P. (December 25, 2010). From Trail to Jail, it Takes Just 3 Months. The Hindu (News daily).

- Bhushan, C. (Feb 1-15, 2012). Growth and risk. Science & Environment Fortnightly, (p. 27).

- Blackburn, K., Neanidis, C. K., & Haque, M. (2009). Corruption, Seignorage and Growth: Theory and Evidence. Center of Growth and Business Cycles Research, Economic Studies, University of Manchester, UK.

- Box, S. (1983). Power, Crime and Mystification. London, UK: Routledge.

- Brinkerhoff, D.W. (2000). Assessing Political will for Anti-corruption Efforts: An Analytic Framework. Public Administration and Development, 20 (3), (pp. 239-252).

- Buscaglia, E & Dijk, J.V. (December 2003). Controlling organized crime and corruption in the public sector. Forum on Crime and Society. 3 (1 & 2), (pp.3- 34).

- Castells, M. (2000). The Information Age: Economy, Society and Culture – The Power of Identity. Oxford: Blackwell.

- Central Bureau of Investigation (2012). A Brief History of CBI. Retrieved 24 July, 2012 from http://www.cbi.gov.in/history.php.
- Central Bureau of Investigation (2012a). Retrieved 24 July, 2012 from http://www.cbi.gov.in/annualreport/cbi_annual_report_2011.pdf.
- Chockalingham, K. (2003). Criminal Victimization in Four Major Cities in Southern India. Forum on Crime and Society. 3 (1 and 2), (p. 117).
- Chopra, S. (4 August 2009). Ethics—Corruption-You can say no to it. Retrieved 25 September, 2009 from http://www.lifepositive.com/Mind/ethics-and-values/ethics/corruption.asp
- Clive, R. (1859). Baron of Plassey- 'Clive of India'. (1725-74). English general and colonial administrator. Originally published in 1859: The British Library Board, (p. 791).
- Cloward, R. A., & Ohlin, L. E. (1960). Delinquency and Opportunity. USA, New York: Free Press.
- CNN-IBN & CNBC-TV18 (August 9, 2011). Corruption is the Big Issue. The Hindu (News daily), (p. 9).
- Cohen, D.V. (1995). Ethics and Crime in Business Firms: Organizational Culture and the Impact of Anomie. Retrieved 24 July, 2012 from https://www.ncjrs.gov/App/publications/Abstract.aspx?id=15963.
- Council of Europe, (2000). Preamble to the Criminal Law Convention of Corruption.
- Cover Story, (Jan 2011). Long shadow of the Radia Tapes. Media Voice, (p. 16).
- Coxson, S. L. (2009). Assessment of Armenian Local Government Corruption Potential. Public Administration and Development, 29 (3), (pp. 193-203).
- Crimes in India, (2011). Retrieved 24 July, 2012 from http://ncrb.gov.in/. (pp. 491-494).
- Crimes in India, (2014). Retrieved 29 July, 2014 from http://ncrb.gov.in/CD-CII2013/home.asp 2013. (pp. 491-494).
- D' Souza, A. (9-15 Jan, 2012). Comment on LokPal. India Currents, (p. 35).
- Dayal, J. (12-18 Sep, 2011). The Saffron Doubles-Speak. India Currents, (p. 26).
- Devarajan, K.M. (21 Jan, 2006). Corruption Conversion. The Statesman, (p.13).
- DH news, (2005). 11 MP's Shame Democracy. Deccan Herald, (p.5).
- Dikshit, S. (December 3, 2010). Its landmark year of scams says CPI (M). The Hindu (News daily), (p. 13).

- Directorate of Vigilance and Anti-Corruption (2012). Retrieved 24 July, 2012 from http://www.dvac.tn.gov.in/.
- Dutta, A. (August 24, 2011). Corruption a part of the prevailing Social Order. The Hindu (News daily), (p. 14).
- Dutta, I. (August 23, 2012). Lokpal will help, but will not solve corruption. The Hindu (News daily), (p. 12).
- Editors, (Sep-Oct 2004). Advocacy Internet, IV (5), (p. 1).
- Eigen, P. (Sep-Oct 2004). India's Corruption Note Book. Advocacy Internet, IV (5), (p.13).
- Felix, R.R., (2011). The Rally. Chennai, India: AICUF, (p. 13).
- Friedman, L.M. (2002). American Law in the Twentieth Century. New Haven, US: Yale University Press, (p.736).
- Friedman, M., & Friedman, R. D. (2002). Capitalism and Freedom. Chicago, US: University of Chicago Press.
- Gupta, K.N. (2001). Corruption in India. New Delhi, India, Anmol Publications Pvt.Ltd (pp. 98-107).
- Gupta, Y.P. (18 Apr, 2001). Academic Scams. The Statesman, (p. 12).
- Gupta, Y.P. (14 Sep, 2007). Cancer at the Core. The Statesman, (p.13).
- Hanlon, J., & Pettifor, A. (2000). Kicking the Habit, Finding a lasting solution to addictive lending and borrowing-and its corrupting side-effects. London: UK. Jubilee Research. Retrieved 25 August, 2014 from http://www.globalissues.org/article/ 590/ corruption
- Hayek, F. A. (2001). The Road to Serfdom. New York, US: Routledge.
- Historical Events at a Glance (2012). Retrieved 29 May, 2012 from http://www.chennai.tn.nic.in/chnhistevents.htm.
- Hunt, E.F., & Colander, D.C. (1999). Social Science 10th Ed. USA: Allyn & Bacon, (pp. 400-01 & 410-12).
- Iyer, V. R. K. (1984). Indian Justice: Perspectives and Problem. Indore, India: Vedpal Law House, (p. 30).
- Jaishankar, K. (2007). What ails criminology education in India?. Souvenir of Meeting of Vice-chancellors of Tamil Nadu State Universities. Tirunelveli, Tamil Nadu: Manonmaniam Sundaranar University.
- Jayawickrama, N. (Sep-Oct 2004). Corruption and Human Rights. Advocacy Internet, VI(5), (p. 2).

- Jha, P. S. (23 Dec, 2012). Clarity Begins at Home. The Hindustan Times, (p. 11).

- JhunJhunwala, B. (29 Apr, 2006). Why more Corruption in India. The New Indian Express, (p. 11).

- Johnston, M. (Sep-Oct 2004). Cross-Border Corruption. Advocacy Internet, VI (5), (p. 25).

- Johnston, M. (2005). Syndromes of Corruption: Wealth, Power, and Democracy. UK: Cambridge: Cambridge University Press.

- Jose, T. (22-28 Nov, 2010). Adarsh in Aberration. India Currents, (p. 37).

- Kalshian, R. (Sep-Oct 2004). India's Corruption Note Book. Advocacy Internet, VI (5), (p. 5).

- Karat, P. (July 23, 2015). Both UPA, BJP indulged in practices, they're no different: corrupt. Retrieved 25 July, 2015 from http://indianexpress.com/article/india/politics/ bjp-govt-no-different-from-upa-regarding-corruption-prakash-karat/.

- Kaushish, P. (March 27, 2012). Business of Governance: Goodbye Sleaze, VIP Security. Retrieved 25 June, 2012 from http://www.sarkaritel.com/business-of-governance-goodbye-sleaze-vip-security, (p. 1).

- Kenny, C. (2006). Measuring and Reducing the Impact of Corruption in Infrastructure. World Bank Policy Research Working Paper 4099, (p.5). Retrieved 22 July, 2012 from http://siteresources.worldbank.org/INTINFNETWORK/Resources /wps4099.pdf.

- Kumar, R. (23 Dec, 2005). Corruption Undermines Democracy Governance. The Hindu, (p. 6).

- Kumar, D. (2012). Notes on some of the Remedial measures since Independence. Retrieved 15 June, 2012 from http://www.preservearticles.com/2011092714235 /notes-on-some-of-the-remedial-measures-since-independence-india.html.

- Laxmikanth, T. (2001). Governance in India (For UPSC Preliminary Examinations-Paper I). India: McGraw-Hill Education (India) Pvt Limited. (p. 5).

- Lee-Chai, A. Y., Chen, S., and Chartrand, T. (2002). From Moses to Marcos: Individual Differences in the Use and Abuse of Power. In Lee-Chai, A. Y., & Bargh J. A. (eds.). The Use and Abuse of Power: Multiple Perspectives on the Causes of Corruption. (pp. 57-71) New York, US: Psychology Press.

- Leighton, D. (1902). Vicissitudes of Fort Saint George. Madras & Bombay, India: A. A. J. Cambridge & Co, (p. 5).

- Lovely, A. S. (August 9, 2011). No indictment of CM or Ministers in CAG report. The Hindu (News daily), (p. 10).

- Mauro, P. (August. 1995). Corruption and Growth. Quarterly Journal of Economics, 110, (pp. 681-712).

- McGettigan, T. (2008). Anomaly Overload: An Evolutionary Theory of Truth. Theory & Science.

- McLennan, G. (2000). 'The New Positivity', in J. Eldridge et al., For Sociology: Legacies and Prospects. Durham, UK: Sociology Press.

- Menon, M. (25, 26 and 27 of February 2009). Special Address. 3rd International and 32nd All India conference of the Indian society of Criminology, Bangalore.

- Menon, P. (24-30 Oct, 2011). States go soft on corruption. India Currents, (p. 14).

- Merton, R. (1957). Social Theory and Social Structure. New York: Free Press (Revised edition).

- Minwalla, S. (21 Jan, 2003). Corruption Rife in Medical Exam. The Times of India.

- Muthukumaran, S. (19 Jun, 2003). Stem the rot within. The Telegraph, (p. 11).

- Naim, M. (1995). Corruption Eruption. In Naunihal (1998). The World of Bribery and Corruption- from Ancient Times to Modern age. New Delhi, India: Mittal Publications.

- Naunihal, S. (1998). The World of Bribery and Corruption- from Ancient Times to Modern age. New Delhi, India: Mittal Publications.

- NCAS, (2004). Globalization and Corruption. Advocacy Internet, VI (5), (p. 23).

- NDTV, (August 26, 2009). 'Big fish' must not escape punishment: PM. Retrieved 18 August, 2013 from http://www.ndtv.com/india-news/big-fish-must-not-escape-punishment-pm-400340.

- Neild, R. (2002). Public Corruption; The Dark Side of Social Evolution, London: Anthem Press.

- Nelken, D. (1994). 'White-Collar Crime'. In: M. Maguire, R. Morgan & R. Reiner (eds.) The Oxford Handbook of Criminology. Oxford: Oxford University Press, (pp. 355-392).

- Noonam, J.T. Jr. (1984). Bribes. New York, US: Macmillan.

- Ojeili, C. E. & Hayden, P. (2006). Critical Theories of Globalization. UK: Palgrave MacMillan, (pp. 2-3 & 190).

- Passas, N. (1998). Structural Analysis of Corruption: The Role of Criminogenic Asymmetries. Transnational Organized Crime, 4(1), (pp. 42-55).

- Pathak, A. (27 Nov, 2003). All Pervasive Corruption. Deccan Herald, (p. 11).

- Philip, A. J. (22-28 Nov, 2010). Height of Corruption. India Currents, (p. 32).

- Plathotham, G. (12-18 Sep, 2011). Eliminate Corruption ensure Governance. India Currents, (p. 20).

- Political Corruption. net, (2010). Types of Corruption Found in Local Government. Retrieved 12 September 2010 from http://www.politicalcorruption.net/2009/01/30/types-of-corruption-found-in-local-government/.
- Puri, R. (25 Oct, 2006). Hidden Sting in Govt's Closet. The Statesman, (p. 8).
- Rabade, P. (15 Jun, 2003). Scam unplugged. Deccan Herald, (p. 3).
- Raghavan, R. K. (December 17, 2010). Case for an Autonomous CBI. The Hindu (News daily).
- Raj, F. (15 Mar, 2005). Social Values-II. The Statesman, (p. 5).
- Ravindra, A. (14 Dec, 2003). Crime, Police and Policing. The New Indian Express, (p. 7).
- Roy, A. (July, 2011). People's Union for Civil Liberties, 8 (9), (p. 23).
- Samimi, A.J., & Abedini, M. (March, 2011). Corruption and Inflation Tax in the Middle East and North Africa (MENA) Region: Sensitivity to Definition of Corruption. Journal of Social and Development Sciences, 1(2), (pp. 67-73).
- Santhanam, K. (1964). Report of the Committee on Prevention of Corruption. New Delhi: Government of India Press, (p. 7).
- Saumitra, M. (9 Nov, 2004). The Skill Game-II. The Statesman, (p. 9).
- Sen, A. (9-15 Jan, 2012). Comment on LokPal. India Currents, (p. 32).
- Sen, S. (8 Jun, 2004). Suspect Bureaucracy-II. The Statesman, (p. 6).
- Sengupta, U. (5 Nov, 2003). Stem the rot within. The Telegraph, (p. 11).
- Shailendra, B.J. (12-18 Sep, 2011). Honesty the best Policy. India Currents, (p. 24).
- Shah, A. (29 December, 2008). Corruption. Retrieved 12 September, 2009 from http://www.globalissues.org/article/590/corruption.
- Singh, K. (25 May, 2006). India & Pak; Corruption tales. The Hindustan Times, (p. 7).
- Singh, M.M. (Kolkata, August 22, 2011). Manmohan: clean up we must, but Lokpal won't solve problem. Retrieved 18 October, 2013 from http://www.thehindu.com/news/national/manmohan-clean-up-we-must-but-lokpal-wont-solve-problem/article2382907.ece.
- Sreevatsan, A. (10 September, 2009). The Hindu (Daily).
- Srivastava, K. (July, 2011). Street Power has its Limits. People's Union for Civil Liberties, (p. 21).
- Sutherland, E. H. (1949). White Collar Crime. New York, USA: Dryden Press.
- Sutherland, E. H. (1961). White Collar Crime. New York, USA: Holt, Rinehart and Winston.

- Sykes, G.M. & Matza, D. (1957). Techniques of Neutralization: A theory of delinquency. American Sociological Review, 22, (pp. 664-70).

- Talukdar, S.P. (9-15 Jan, 2012). Election Time; More Sops; No Agenda. India Currents, (p. 30).

- Thakur, A.K. (7 Jun, 2003). Corruption Thrives in Coal Industry. The Times of India, (p. 7).

- Thakur, P., & Das, S. (11 Oct, 2009). Jharkhand former CM amassed Rs. 400 Crores Assets. The Times of India, (p. 10).

- Thamilarasan, M., & Venkatesan, G. (2011). Human Rights and Corruption. Souvenir of National Seminar on Corruption and Human Rights, (p. 84).

- Thampu, V. (26 Jul, 2003). Who will bell the Cat. Deccan Herald, (p. 3).

- The Global Corruption Barometer, (2004). Transparency International. Retrieved 16 July, 2012 from http://cpi.transparency.org/.

- The Prevention of Corruption Act, (1988). Definitions. Retrieved 05 February, 2012 from http://www.vakilno1.com/bareacts/Prevofcorrup /S2.htm.

- Thiminappa, K. (20 Jun, 2003). Pernicious Practices. Deccan Herald, (p. 11).

- Top Scams in India, (2010). Retrieved 05 February 2012 from http://trak.in/tags/ business/2010/11/25/top-10-corruption-scams-scandals-india/.

- Trace International (2009). Retrieved 24 July, 2012 from https://secure. traceinternational.org/index.html.

- Transparency International, (2011). Retrieved 15 July, 2012 from http://cpi.transparency.org/cpi2011/results/.

- Transparency International, (2012). Retrieved 05 February, 2012 from http://www. transparency.org/whoweare/organisation/faqs_on_corruption

- Transparency International, (2014). Retrieved 05 July, 2014 from http://www. transparency.org/cpi2014/results#myAnchor1

- Trocchi, A. (1966). Cain's Book. London, UK: Jupiter Books.

- Tummala, K. K. (2009). Combating Corruption: Lessons Out of India. International Public Management Network, 10 (1).

- Umarhathab, S. (Apr- Jun, 2007). Public Rating of Corruption. The Indian Police Journal, LIV (2), (pp. 82-95).

- Umarhathab, S. & Kumar, S. R. (May-December 2009). Understanding Corruption at Grassroot-A Study on Public Views on Corrupt Departments, Their Participation and Victimization. The Indian Journal of Criminology & Criminalistics, XXX (2 & 3), (P. 94).

- Umarhathab, S. (2011). Combating Corruption in India: Major threats. In V.N. Vishwanathan (Eds.) Corruption and Human Rights, Delhi, India: Allied publishers Pvt Ltd. (PP. 79-83)

- Union Financial Budget (2012-13). Impact on the Power sector. Retrieved on 25.06.2012 from http://www.grantthornton.in/html/budget/2012-13/ind/ Budget _2012- 13_Impact_on_Power_sector.pdf. (p. 3).

- Venkatesan. G. (August 28, 2009). First Step towards Judges Accountability. The Hindu (News daily).

- Vian, T., Brinkerhoff, D.W., Feeley, F.G., Salomon, M., & Vien, N.T.K. (2012). Confronting corruption in the health sector in Vietnam: Patterns and prospects. Public Administration and Development, 32 (1), (pp 49-63).

- Vir, J.R. (2006). Crime and Corruption in India. India: New Delhi, Friends publishing house.

- Vittal, N. (30 Nov, 2003). Who's afraid of corruption?. The New Indian Express, (p.7).

- Wahitha, A. (2011). Human Rights and Corruption. Souvenir of National Seminar on Corruption and Human Rights, (pp. 82-83).

- Werlin, H. H. (1973). The Consequences of Corruption: The Ghanaian Experience, Political Science Quarterly, 88 (1), (pp. 71-85).

- World Bank. (1997). World Development Report: The State in a Changing World. New York: Oxford University Press.

- World Bank. (2012). Introduction to Corruption. Youth for Good Governance- distance learning program. Retrieved 25 April, 2014 from http://img.modernghana.com/ images/content/report_content/youthforgoodgovernance.pdf.

- Zimring, F. E., & Johnson, D.T. (2005). On the comparative study of corruption. British Journal of Criminology, 45, (pp. 793-809).

Details of Corporation

1. Chennai- www.chennaicorporation.gov.in
2. Coimbatore- https://www.ccmc.gov.in/
3. Erode- http://erodecorporation.gov.in/
4. Madurai- http://203.101.40.168/newmducorp/
5. Salem- www.salemcorporation.gov.in/
6. Tirunelveli- http://www.tirunelvelicorporation.in/

7.   Tiruppur- http://tiruppur.tn.nic.in/

8.   Trichy- www.trichycorporation.gov.in/

9.   Tuticorin- http://thoothukudi.nic.in/

10. Vellore- http://www.vellore.tn.nic.in/govtoff.htm

LIST OF ABBREVIATIONS

2G Scam- Distribution of 2G spectrum scam

ADB- Asian Developmental Bank

AFDB- African Developmental Bank

AVD- Administrative Vigilance Division

CAG- The Comptroller Auditor General of India

CBI- Central Bureau of Investigation

CIC- The Central Information Commission

CPI- Corruption Perception Index

CrPC- Criminal Procedure Code of India

CVC- Central Vigilance Commission

DSPE- Delhi Special Police Establishment

DV and AC- Directorate of Vigilance and Anti- Corruption

EB- Electricity Board

EOW- Economic Offences Wing

GOW- General Offences Wing

GPH- Government Public Hospitals/ Primary health center

ICCPR- International Covenant on Civil and Political Rights, 1966

ICESCR- International Covenant on Economic, Social and Cultural Rights

IO- Investigation officer

IPC- Indian Penal Code

IPL Scam- Indian Premier League scam

JNNSM- Jawaharlal Nehru National Solar Mission

Judiciary- Judges/Magistrate, Public Prosecutor, Defense Counsel and Courts

MLA Member of Legislatives Assembly

MP- Member of Parliament

NA- Mean's data not available

NCRB- National Crime Records Bureau

OC- Others communications

PDS- Public Distribution System (Ration Shops, Free Distribution Saree, Dhotis, Television sets, Mixing Grinders, Goats, Milchi cow)

PO- Personal Opinion

Police- Crime, Traffic, Law and Order

PSU- Public Sector Undertaking

PWD- Public Works Department

Railways- Indian/Southern any other zonal operator of India

RD- Revenue Department (Office of the Corporation, Tehsil office, Block Development Office, Office of the Revenue Inspector)

RDA- Regular Departmental Action

RO- Register Office (Land/ Marriages/ Patta and etc.)

Rs- Rupees

RTO- Regional Transport Office

SCRA- Securities Contract Regulation Act, 1956

TI- Transparency International

Trust- Trust/ Missionaries/ Welfare society/ Non-Governmental Organization

UN- United Nation

UNCAC- United Nation Convention against Corruption

WEF- World Economic Forum

Table A 1: Public Ranking of the Public Sectors

➡ Rank ▼ Name of the Public Sectors	1	2	3	4	5	Total	Rank
Police (Crime, traffic, law and order)	223	140	135	167	99	764	1
Register office	162	133	130	81	93	599	2 & 3
Revenue department	116	140	111	99	93	559	2 & 3
Public work department (PWD)	98	115	103	81	118	515	6
Regional transport office (RTO)	91	123	105	88	69	476	7
Public distribution system	90	103	116	125	122	556	4
Government Public Hospitals (GPH)	51	49	77	93	85	355	7
Judiciary (Judges/Magistrate, public prosecutor and courts)	51	67	47	64	50	279	10
Electricity board (EB)	49	54	58	88	98	347	8
Taxation	36	50	81	57	77	301	9
Railways (Indian/Southern any other zonal operator of India)	25	10	26	23	55	139	11
Trust /Missionaries/ Welfare society/ Ngo's	8	16	11	34	41	110	12

ANNEXURE II

Table A 2: Scams and Public Ranking

List of Scams	1	2	3	4	5	Total	Rank
2G Spectrum scam (Raja)	709	97	59	40	40	945	1
Bofors scam (Congress)	80	173	95	81	84	513	4
IPL Scam (Lalit Modi)	56	133	191	152	176	708	3
Commonwealth games scam (Suresh Kalmadi)	39	274	259	127	81	780	2
Stamp paper scam (Telgi)	36	51	68	115	123	393	7
Satyam Scam (Ramalinga Raju)	25	98	98	135	94	450	5
Insurance fraud (Harshad Mehta Ketan)	18	68	102	112	95	395	6
Hawala scandal (Hasan Ali)	14	48	40	86	141	329	8
Fodder scam (Lalu Prasad Yadav)	12	24	73	93	113	315	9
Stock market scam (Parekh)	11	34	15	59	53	172	10

Coimbatore Data- Frequency tables of the Study

Table 1: Socio-demographic Variables of the Respondents

Options	n	%	Options	n	%
Age in years			**Educational qualification**		
<=20	37	37.0	Until class 10	4	4.0
>20<=30	26	26.0	> 10-12 class	18	18
>30<=40	10	10.0	ITI / Dip	7	7.0
>40	27	27.0	Graduate's and above	67	67.0
Sex			Other specify	4	4.0
Male	72	72.0	**Marital Status**		
Female	28	28.0	Single	57	57.0
Income in Rupees			Married	38	38.0
<=10000	52	52.0	Divorced	4	4.0
> 10000 <= 25000	28	28.0	widow	1	1.0
> 25000 <= 50000	14	14.0	**Family types**		
> 50000	6	6.0	Joint Family	22	22.0
			Nuclear Family	68	68.0
			Living Alone	9	9.0
			Other specify	1	1.0

Table 2: The Respondent's and their Father's Occupation

Options	n	%	Options	n	%
Respondent' s occupation			**Father' s occupation**		
Student	54	54.0	Business	10	10.0
Business	7	7.0	Daily wage labour	13	13.0
Govt. employee	4	4.0	Govt. employee	14	14.0
Private employee	9	9.0	Private employee	12	12.0
Home maker	6	6.0	Home maker	1	1.0
Teacher/faculty	2	2.0	Teacher/faculty	-	-
Own Profession	5	5.0	Own Profession	10	10.0
Agarian	-	-	Agarian	14	14.0
Retired person	10	10.0	Retired person	14	14.0
Other specify	3	3.0	Other specify	12	12.0

Table 3: Public Rating of the Public Sectors with Rank

Rank	1	2	3	4	5	Total	Rank
Police (Crime, traffic, law and order)	25	16	7	9	10	67	1
Judiciary (Judges/Magistrate, public prosecutor and courts)	13	12	8	10	7	50	5
Revenue department	11	13	18	8	13	63	3
Public distribution system	10	3	13	17	8	51	4
Register office	10	17	17	14	8	66	2
Taxation	9	8	11	9	6	43	6
Public work department (PWD)	6	10	2	5	14	37	7
Government Public Hospitals (GPH)	5	2	5	9	7	28	10
Regional transport office (RTO)	5	13	4	4	6	32	9
Trust /Missionaries/ Welfare society/ Ngo's	5	1	3	1	5	15	11
Electricity board (EB)	1	4	8	13	10	36	8
Railways (Indian/Southern any other zonal operator of India)	-	1	4	1	6	12	12
	100	100	100	100	100	500	

Table 4: Basis of the Public Ranking of the Public Sectors and Media Influence

Options	n	%	Options	n	%
Basis of the public rating			**Media influence**		
Personal experience	59	59.0	Yes	64	64.0
Other experience	17	17.0	No	18	18.0
Media	24	24.0	Not Sure	18	18.0

Table 5: Public Interest on Corruption during their Routines

Options	Yes	No	Not sure
Interested in reading the articles published in dailies	68	23	9
Interested in reading the articles published in weeklies	63	28	9
Follow news articles related to corruption on a regular basis	53	38	9
Interested in listening to the news related to corruption in radio	41	50	9
Interested in watching news relating to corruption in television	82	9	9
Followed the articles on corruption published by Wiki leaks	37	44	19
In your opinion do media play a prominent role in whistle blowing?	69	12	19
Media cover only the corruption at higher levels of government?	37	33	30
Media cover only the corruption at local levels of government?	26	38	36

Table 6: Corruption-First Thing that Comes to Participant's Minds

Options	n	%	Options	n	%
Politician	61	61.0	**Above Experience based**		
Government sector	37	37.0	Personal experience	27	27.0
Private offices/ companies/ schools	2	2.0	Other experience	10	10.0
			Media	61	61.0
			Other Specify	2	2.0

Table 7: Public Personalities and Corruption – Participant's Opinion

Name of the personality	Corruption committed	Prevent corruption	Not Sure	How did you know			
				PO*	OC#	Media	
						Yes	No
Ramalinga Raju	65	7	28	-	16	69	15
Raja	98	-	2	2	19	79	-
Kiranbedi	11	62	27	2	18	66	14
KaniMozhi	95	1	4	1	19	79	1
Harshad mehtha	53	10	37	-	18	66	16
Prasad bhusan	16	28	56	-	17	59	24
Dayanithi Maran	83	3	14	1	16	78	5

PO* - personal Opinion

OC# - Other communication

Table 8: Top Scams and Public Ranking

List of Scams	1	2	3	4	5	Total	Rank
2G Spectrum scam (Raja)	63	8	9	8	4	92	1
Bofors scam (Congress)	12	19	9	8	16	64	2
IPL Scam (Lalit Modi)	6	6	21	10	11	54	4
Insurance fraud (Harshad Mehta Ketan)	5	8	11	13	12	49	5
Satyam Scam (Ramalinga Raju)	4	13	9	7	10	43	6
Stamp paper scam (Telgi)	3	6	11	10	10	40	7
Commonwealth games scam (Suresh Kalmadi)	2	22	17	9	9	59	3
Fodder scam (Lalu Prasad Yadav)	2	3	6	17	10	38	8
Hawala scandal (Hasan Ali)	2	6	7	10	11	36	9
Stock market scam (Parekh)	1	9	-	8	7	25	10
	100	100	100	100	100	500	

Table 9: Your above Rating based on

	Frequency	Percent
Personal experience	14	14.0
Other experience	8	8.0
Media	78	78.0
Total		

Table 10: Public Interest in Fighting Corruption

Options	n	%	Options	n	%
Interested in fighting corruption			**Corruption as a problem**		
Yes	79	79.0	Local	1	1.0
No	9	9.0	Regional/ District	2	2.0
Not Sure	12	12.0	State	1	1.0
			National	43	43.0
			International	53	53.0

Table 11: Top Reasons of Corruption and Public Ranking

List of reasons for corruption	1	2	3	4	5	Total	Rank
Paid for an illegal work/entity to done	19	11	14	8	10	62	3
Urgentness of issue	18	5	18	13	9	63	2
Don' t like to spend much time in govt. offices	11	16	5	8	11	51	5
Do not know the formalities to complain	11	4	8	9	12	44	7
Bribe demanding office setup	11	14	11	15	14	65	1
Fearlessness of govt. staff towards the action against corruption	9	8	9	10	15	51	6
Individual laziness	8	14	12	9	10	53	4
Rotten system	4	12	4	8	5	33	9
Unaware of formalities	4	3	4	10	2	23	10
Low payment to govt. staff	3	4	4	1	5	17	11
Weak vigilance and anticorruption agency	2	9	11	9	7	38	8
	100	100	100	100	100	500	

Table 12: Your above Rating Based on

	Frequency	Percent
Personal experience	55	55.0
Other experience	17	17.0
Media	28	28.0

Table 13: Appreciating an Act of Corruption by the Participants

During our course of occupation	Yes	No	Not sure
Favoring our neighbors amounts to corruption	70	14	16
Favoring our relatives amounts to corruption	74	14	12
Favoring our best friend amounts to corruption	72	14	14
Using government properties such as using telephone for personnel use will amount to corruption	75	11	14
Using government properties such as using Xerox copier for personnel use will amount to corruption	74	13	13
Using government services such as telephone for personnel use will amount to corruption	73	10	17
Using government properties such as computers for personnel use will amount to corruption	67	12	21
Using government properties such as internet services for personnel use will amount to corruption	70	13	17

Table 14: Respondents Participation in Corruption and Reasons

Options	n	%	Options	n	%
Is bribing a crime			**Bribed making work done**		
Yes	96	96.0	Yes	74	74.0
No	3	3.0	No	25	25.0
Not Sure	1	1.0	Not Sure	1	1.0
Was that a demand? (n=74)			**Was that for doing a legal thing/entity (n=74)**		
Yes	52	70.3	Yes	14	18.9
No	7	9.4	No	41	55.4
Not Sure	15	20.3	Not Sure	19	25.7
Interested in complaining the corruption cases			**Would like to be part of social bribing system**		
Yes	66	66.0	Yes	55	55.0
No	13	13.0	No	32	32.0
Not Sure	21	21.0	Not Sure	13	13.0
Support the corruption in public sector			**If yes, can corruption be decriminalize (n=26)**		
Yes	25	25.0	Yes	11	42.30
No	61	61.0	No	15	57.7
Not Sure	14	14.0	Not Sure	-	-

Table 15: Respondents Experience and Corruption (n= 46)

Was that to achieve following birth rights?	Yes	No	Not sure
For community certificate	40	32	2
For getting driving license	38	34	2
For income corticated	37	36	1
For complaint the police station	34	37	3
For birth certificate	33	40	1
For ration card	28	45	1
For death certificate	28	46	-
For getting treatment in government hospitals	22	48	4
For TNGST/CST no	19	51	4
For getting scholarship	18	53	3

Table 16: Reporting behaviour and Reasons for Not- reporting

Options	Yes	No	Not sure
Attempted to complain on the event of corruption	15	84	1
Seen any officer being bribed	86	14	-
Yes (n=86) Made a complaint to the authorities	15	71	-
Action taken against the complaint (n=15)	6	9	-
Were you happy about the action (n=6)	3	3	-
Rejection of complaint was informed (n=9)	1	8	-
Reason for not reporting the corruption (n=71)			
Unwillingness	33	28	10
Police will act on their own	10	55	6
No faith in police	40	28	3
Don't know whom to report	30	39	2
Fear of reverse action	40	28	3
Problem in witnessing	41	28	2
Fear of police	33	35	3
No action will be taken	50	17	4
Waste of time	39	30	2
Fear/shame	30	38	3

Table 17: Participants Awareness on the Government Measures to Fight Corruption and RTI

Options	Yes	No	Not sure
Aware of department of the vigilance and anti corruption (V & AC)?	71	5	4
Aware of the contact address of the office of the V & AC	20	72	8
Aware of the phone numbers of the office of the V & AC?	19	73	8
Aware of the prevention of the corruption act?	34	59	7
Does it deal with corruption in public services? (n=34)	14	11	9
The Right to Information (RTI) Act, 2005			
Aware of the Right to information (RTI) act, 2005?	48	52	-
The right to information act was enacted to ......? (n=48) • To achieve our birth rights.	20	23	5
• To fix accountability and ensure transparency in government working	35	11	2
• T o eliminate corruption and bribe in public bodies.	29	14	5
Ever used RTI? (n=48)	17	31	-
Was the attempt a successful one? (n=17)	12	5	-
Yes, it was a successful attempt (n=5) • Personal interest and satisfaction	1	3	1
• Public cause	2	3	-
• Benefit of others	2	2	1

Table 18: Awareness on RTI by the Respondents and their Experience

Options	n	%	Options	n	%
Knowledge of the RTI act, 2005 (n=48)			**Came across success story of winning issues through RTI (n=48)**		
Personnel experience	5	10.4	Yes	39	81.3
Other experience	18	37.5	**Source of knowledge on success stories (n=39)**		
Media	25	52.1	Personal experience	4	10.2
			Other experience	20	51.3
			Media	15	38.5

Table 19: Knowledge of Lok Pal and Jan Lok Pal Bill

Options	n	%	Options	n	%
Aware of Lok Pal Bill			**Aware of Jan Lok Pal Bill**		
Yes	78	78.0	Yes	50	50.0
No	18	18.0	No	43	43.0
Not Sure	4	4.0	Not Sure	7	7.0
Lok Pal Empowered with	**Yes**	**Not sure**	**Lok Pal Empowered with**	**Yes**	**Not sure**
To punish politician	63	3	To punish politician	46	5
To punish state government servant	52	7	To punish state government servant	37	8
To punish central government servant	56	7	To punish central government servant	41	7
To punish all who are corrupt	62	5	To punish all who are corrupt	40	6
To increase the investigation agency's power	47	11	To increase the investigation agency's power	32	7
To control lower level corruption	52	10	To control lower level corruption	35	8
To control higher level corruption	58	7	To control higher level corruption	35	7
To control all forms of corruption	63	7	To control all forms of corruption	41	7

Erode Data- Frequency Tables of the Study

Table 1: Socio-Demographic Variables of the Respondents

Options	n	%	Options	n	%
Age in years			**Educational qualification**		
<=20	12	12.0	Until class 10	6	6.0
>20<=30	62	62.0	> 10-12 class	8	8.0
>30<=40	16	16.0	ITI / Dip	3	3.0
>40	10	10.0	Graduate's and above	78	78.0
Sex			Other specify	5	5.0
Male	59	59.0	**Marital Status**		
Female	41	41.0	Single	74	74.0
Income in Rupees			Married	26	26.0
<=10000	31	31.0	**Family types**		
> 10000 <= 25000	49	49.0	Joint Family	27	27.0
> 25000 <= 50000	14	14.0	Nuclear Family	68	68.0
> 50000	6	6.0	Living Alone	4	4.0
			Other specify	1	1.0

Table 2: The Respondent's and their Father's Occupation

Options	n	%	Options	n	%
Respondent' s occupation			**Father' s occupation**		
Student	50	50.0	Business	18	18.0
Business	1	1.0	Daily wage labour	6	6.0
Daily wage labour	3	3.0	Govt. employee	25	25.0
Govt. employee	7	7.0	Private employee	10	10.0
Private employee	17	17.0	Home maker	2	2.0
Home maker	5	5.0	Teacher/faculty	1	1.0
Teacher/faculty	1	1.0	Own Profession	10	10.0
Own Profession	9	9.0	Agarian	11	11.0
Agarian	2	2.0	Retired person	12	12.0
Retired person	4	4.0	Other specify	5	5.0
Other specify	1	1.0			

Table 3: Public Rating of the Public Sectors with Rank

Rank	1	2	3	4	5	Total	Rank
Police (Crime, traffic, law and order)	15	16	13	15	15	74	1
Register office	15	11	11	6	12	55	4
Electricity board (EB)	12	-	7	5	9	33	7
Public work department (PWD)	12	8	14	11	10	55	5
Regional transport office (RTO)	12	19	11	10	7	59	2
Revenue department	11	15	10	13	9	58	3
Government Public Hospitals (GPH)	6	10	7	6	9	38	8
Public distribution system	6	7	8	15	14	50	6
Judiciary (Judges/Magistrate, public prosecutor and courts)	4	6	7	4	6	27	9
Taxation	4	4	9	10	5	32	10
Railways (Indian/Southern any other zonal operator of India)	2	2	2	1	4	11	11
Trust /Missionaries/ Welfare society/ Ngo's	1	2	1	4	-		

Table 4: Basis of the Public Ranking of the Public Sectors and Media Influence

Options	n	%	Options	n	%
Basis of the public rating			**Media influence**		
Personal experience	45	45.0	Yes	45	45.0
Other experience	36	36.0	No	28	28.0
Media	19	19.0	Not Sure	27	27.0

Table 5: Public Interest on Corruption during their Routines

Options	Yes	No	Not sure
Interested in reading the articles published in dailies	47	38	15
Interested in reading the articles published in weeklies	47	38	15
Follow news articles related to corruption on a regular basis	43	38	19
Interested in listening to the news related to corruption in radio	40	46	14
Interested in watching news relating to corruption in television	82	6	12
Followed the articles on corruption published by Wiki leaks	29	55	16
In your opinion do media play a prominent role in whistle blowing?	83	7	10
Media cover only the corruption at higher levels of government?	61	27	12
Media cover only the corruption at local levels of government?	37	41	22

Table 6: Corruption – First Thing that Comes to Participants Minds

Options	n	%	Options	n	%
Politician	66	66.0	**Above experience is based**		
Government sector	34	34.0	Personal experience	14	14.0
Private offices/companies/ schools	-	-	Other experience	20	20.0
			Media	66	66.0

Table 7: Famous Public Personalities and Public Options with Reference to Corruption

Name of the personality	Corruption committed	Prevent corruption	Not Sure	How did you know			
				PO*	OC#	Media	
						Yes	No
Raja	88	1	11	-	8	83	9
KaniMozhi	83	-	17	-	5	81	14
Dayanithi Maran	66	-	34	-	4	80	16
Ramalinga Raju	53	4	43	-	9	64	27
Harshad mehtha	44	9	47	-	6	63	31
Prasad bhusan	12	22	66	-	7	55	38
Kiranbedi	6	48	46	-	5	70	25

PO* - Personal Opinion

OC# - Other Communication

Table 8: Top Scams and Public Ranking

List of Scams	1	2	3	4	5	Total	Rank
2G Spectrum scam (Raja)	80	7	5	2	1	95	1
Bofors scam (Congress)	6	30	9	6	6	57	4
Satyam Scam (Ramalinga Raju)	4	13	11	14	8	50	5
Stamp paper scam (Telgi)	4	3	5	5	8	25	8
IPL Scam (Lalit Modi)	3	10	15	14	31	73	3
Commonwealth games scam (Suresh Kalmadi)	2	25	33	16	10	86	2
Insurance fraud (Harshad Mehta Ketan)	1	5	10	18	11	45	6
Stock market scam (Parekh)	-	2	1	9	6	18	10
Fodder scam (Lalu Prasad Yadav)	-	2	7	7	9	25	9
Hawala scandal (Hasan Ali)	-	3	4	9	10	26	7
	100	100	100	100	100	500	

Table 9: Your above rating based on

	Frequency	Percent
Personal experience	12	12.0
Other experience	10	10.0
Media	78	78.0

Table 10: Public Interest in Fighting Corruption

Options	n	%	Options	n	%
Interested in fighting corruption			**Corruption as a problem**		
Yes	70	70.0	Local	1	1.0
No	13	13.0	Regional/ District	1	1.0
Not Sure	17	17.0	State	6	6.0
			National	30	30.0
			International	62	62.0

Table 11: Top Reasons of Corruption and Public Ranking

List of reasons for corruption	1	2	3	4	5	Total	Rank
Paid for an illegal work/entity to done	19	12	19	4	7	61	2
Urgentness of issue	16	10	9	13	14	62	1
Don't like to spend much time in govt. offices	15	10	8	12	11	56	4
Bribe demanding office setup	13	20	7	7	10	57	3
Weak vigilance and anticorruption agency	10	2	15	15	7	49	7
Rotten system	9	9	5	5	10	38	8
Fearlessness of govt. staff towards the action against corruption	6	8	4	7	10	35	9
Individual laziness	6	12	18	9	10	55	5
Do not know the formalities to complain	3	10	9	18	13	53	6
Unaware of formalities	2	6	4	5	5	22	10
Low payment to govt. staff	1	1	2	5	3	12	11

Table 12: Your above Rating Based on

	Frequency	Percent
Personal experience	43	43.0
Other experience	32	32.0
Media	25	25.0

Table 13: Appreciating an Act of Corruption by the Participants

During our course of occupation	Yes	No	Not sure
Favoring our neighbors amounts to corruption	62	27	11
Favoring our relatives amounts to corruption	66	20	14
Favoring our best friend amounts to corruption	64	23	13
Using government properties such as using telephone for personnel use will amount to corruption	66	20	14
Using government properties such as using Xerox copier for personnel use will amount to corruption	66	14	20
Using government services such as telephone for personnel use will amount to corruption	65	17	18
Using government properties such as computers for personnel use will amount to corruption	60	21	19
Using government properties such as internet services for personnel use will amount to corruption	66	16	18

Table 14: Respondent's Participation in Corruption and Reasons

Options	n	%	Options	n	%
Is bribing a crime			**Bribed for making work done**		
Yes	97	97.0	Yes	55	55.0
No	2	2.0	No	39	39.0
Not Sure	1	1.0	Not Sure	6	6.0
Was that a demand? (n=55)			**Was that for doing a legal thing/entity (n=55)**		
Yes	45	81.8	Yes	8	14.6
No	8	14.6	No	40	72.7
Not Sure	2	3.6	Not Sure	7	12.7
Interested in complaining the corruption cases			**Would like to be part of social bribing system**		
Yes	64	64.0	Yes	38	38.0
No	14	14.0	No	40	40.0
Not Sure	22	22.0	Not Sure	22	22.0
Support the corruption in public sector			**If yes, can corruption be decriminalize (n=19)**		
Yes	19	19.0	Yes	5	26.3
No	63	63.0	No	11	57.9
Not Sure	18	18.0	Not Sure	3	15.8

Table 15: Respondents Experience and Corruption (n=55)

Was that to achieve following birth rights?	Yes	No	Not sure
For community certificate	38	16	1
For getting driving license	30	23	2
For income corticated	30	24	1
For birth certificate	25	28	2
For getting treatment in government hospitals	21	30	4
For death certificate	19	32	4
For complaint the police station	19	34	2
For getting scholarship	14	35	6
For TNGST/CST no	11	40	4
For ration card	6	34	5

Table 16: Reporting behaviour and Reasons for Not-reporting

Options	Yes	No	Not sure
Attempted to complain on the event of corruption	9	90	1
Seen any officer being bribed	71	27	2
Yes (n=71) Made a complaint to the authorities	5	66	-
Action taken against the complaint (n=5)	2	3	-
Were you happy about the action (n=2)	1	1	-
Rejection of complaint was informed(n=3)	-	3	-
Reason for not reporting the corruption (n=66)			
Unwillingness	29	33	4
Police will act on their own	9	48	9
No faith in police	21	39	6
Don't know whom to report	22	40	4
Fear of reverse action	24	38	4
Problem in witnessing	25	36	5
Fear of police	26	37	3
No action will be taken	47	13	6
Waste of time	40	21	5
Fear/shame	19	41	6

Table 17: Participants Awareness on the Government Measures to Fight Corruption and RTI

Options	Yes	No	Not sure
Aware of department of the vigilance and anti corruption (**V & AC**)?	77	21	2
Aware of the contact address of the office of the V & AC	18	79	3
Aware of the phone numbers of the office of the V & AC?	10	85	5
Aware of the prevention of the corruption act?	**41**	56	3
Does it deal with corruption in public services? **(n=41)**	14	15	12
The Right to Information (RTI) Act, 2005			
Aware of the Right to information (RTI) act, 2005?	40	60	-
The right to information act was enacted to ......? **(n=40)**	22	8	10
• To achieve our birth rights.			
• To fix accountability and ensure transparency in government working	32	4	4
• T o eliminate corruption and bribe in public bodies.	24	10	6
Ever used RTI? **(n=40)**	9	41	-
Was the attempt a successful one? **(n=9)**	5	2	2
Yes, it was a successful attempt **(n=4)**	1	1	2
• Personal interest and satisfaction			
• Public cause	1	3	-
• Benefit of others	2	1	1

Table 18: Awareness on RTI by the Respondents and their Experience

Options	n	%	Options	n	%
Knowledge of the RTI act, 2005 (n=40)			**Came across success story of winning issues through RTI (n=40)**		
Personnel experience	4	10.0	Yes	28	70.0
Other experience	14	35.0	**Source of knowledge on success stories (n=28)**		
Media	22	55.0	Personal experience	1	3.6
			Other experience	22	78.6
			Media	5	17.8

Table 19: Knowledge of Lok Pal and Jan Lok Pal Bill

Options	n	%	Options	n	%
Aware of Lok Pal Bill			**Aware of Jan Lok Pal Bill**		
Yes	56	56.0	Yes	48	48.0
No	35	35.0	No	39	39.0
Not Sure	9	9.0	Not Sure	13	13.0
Lok Pal Empowered with	**Yes**	**Not sure**	**Lok Pal Empowered with**	**Yes**	**Not sure**
To punish politician	47	3	To punish politician	44	-
To punish state government servant	36	11	To punish state government servant	38	4
To punish central government servant	40	8	To punish central government servant	39	5
To punish all who are corrupt	40	5	To punish all who are corrupt	40	3
To increase the investigation agency's power	25	12	To increase the investigation agency's power	37	4
To control lower level corruption	35	9	To control lower level corruption	39	2
To control higher level corruption	36	9	To control higher level corruption	40	4
To control all forms of corruption	41	6	To control all forms of corruption	41	4

Madurai Data- Frequency Tables of the Study

Table 1: Socio-demographic Variables of the Respondents

Options	n	%	Options	n	%
Age in years			**Educational qualification**		
<=20	29	29.0	Until class 10	19	19.0
>20<=30	23	23.0	> 10-12 class	22	22.0
>30<=40	18	18.0	ITI / Dip	8	8.0
>40	30	30.0	Graduate's and above	46	46.0
Sex			Other specify	5	5.0
Male	51	51.0	**Marital Status**		
Female	49	49.0	Single	41	41.0
Income in Rupees			Married	43	43.0
<=10000	41	41.0	Divorced	8	8.0
> 10000 <= 25000	36	36.0	Widow	6	6.0
> 25000 <= 50000	17	17.0	Other specify	2	2.0
> 50000	6	6.0	**Family types**		
			Joint Family	23	23.0
			Nuclear Family	57	57.0
			Living Alone	18	18.0
			Other specify	2	2.0

Table 2: The respondent's and their Father's Occupation

Options	n	%	Options	n	%
Respondent' s occupation			**Father' s occupation**		
Student	25	25.0	Business	17	17.0
Business	7	7.0	Daily wage labour	12	12.0
Govt. employee	10	10.0	Govt. employee	8	8.0
Private employee	3	3.0	Private employee	9	9.0
Home maker	10	10.0	Home maker	6	6.0
Teacher/faculty	15	15.0	Teacher/faculty	2	2.0
Own Profession	5	5.0	Own Profession	16	16.0
Agarian	18	18.0	Agarian	15	15.0
Retired person	4	4.0	Retired person	10	10.0
Other specify	3	3.0	Other specify	5	5.0

Table 3: Public Rating of the Public Sectors with Rank

Rank	1	2	3	4	5	Total	Rank
Register office	20	11	8	6	16	61	1
Police (Crime, traffic, law and order)	16	14	9	11	10	60	2
Revenue department	14	8	10	10	7	49	4
Public distribution system	13	10	14	10	10	57	3
Public work department (PWD)	11	7	9	7	8	42	6
Government Public Hospitals (GPH)	6	3	7	13	1	30	9
Judiciary (Judges/Magistrate, public prosecutor and courts)	6	16	5	6	9	42	7
Regional transport office (RTO)	6	3	5	3	5	22	12
Railways (Indian/Southern any other zonal operator of India)	4	2	10	6	5	27	10
Electricity board (EB)	3	12	10	9	9	43	5
Taxation	1	7	12	6	15	41	8
Trust /Missionaries/ Welfare society/ Ngo's	-	7	1	13	5	26	11
	100	100	100	100	100	500	

Table 4: Basis of the Public Ranking of the Public Sectors and Media Influence

Options	n	%	Options	n	%
Basis of the public rating			**Media influence**		
Personal experience	36	36.0	Yes	64	64.0
Other experience	29	29.0	No	21	21.0
Media	35	35.0	Not Sure	15	15.0

Table 5: Public Interest on Corruption during their Routines

Options	Yes	No	Not sure
Interested in reading the articles published in dailies	52	39	9
Interested in reading the articles published in weeklies	41	53	6
Follow news articles related to corruption on a regular basis	47	46	7
Interested in listening to the news related to corruption in radio	30	59	11
Interested in watching news relating to corruption in television	73	26	1
Followed the articles on corruption published by Wiki leaks	33	59	8
In your opinion do media play a prominent role in whistle blowing?	63	22	15
Media cover only the corruption at higher levels of government?	37	37	26
Media cover only the corruption at local levels of government?	39	28	33

Table 6: Corruption – First thing that Comes to Participant's Minds

Options	n	%	Options	n	%
Politician	69	69.0	**Above experienced is based on**		
Government sector	29	29.0	Personal experience	11	11.0
Private offices/ companies/ schools	2	2.0	Other experience	18	18.0
			Media	69	69.0
			Other Specify	2	2.0

Table 7: Public Personalities and Corruption – Participant's Opinion

Name of the personality	Corruption committed	Prevent corruption	Not Sure	PO*	OC#	Media	
						Yes	No
Raja	81	4	15	2	17	69	12
KaniMozhi	81	4	15	2	14	71	13
Dayanithi Maran	71	3	26	2	16	66	16
Harshad mehtha	60	7	33	2	14	64	20
Ramalinga Raju	53	5	42	2	16	59	23
Kiranbedi	28	38	34	2	16	58	24
Prasad bhusan	23	26	51	2	13	57	28

PO*   Personal opinion

OC# – Other Communication

Table 8: Top Scams and Public Ranking

List of Scams	1	2	3	4	5	Total	Rank
2G Spectrum scam (Raja)	50	13	11	16	5	95	1
Bofors scam (Congress)	12	14	12	10	8	56	3
IPL Scam (Lalit Modi)	11	18	8	12	16	65	2
Stamp paper scam (Telgi)	10	5	5	14	14	48	6
Insurance fraud (Harshad Mehta Ketan)	5	10	9	7	8	39	8
Commonwealth games scam (Suresh Kalmadi)	4	12	16	11	8	51	4
Stock market scam (Parekh)	4	5	4	2	6	21	10
Satyam Scam (Ramalinga Raju)	2	13	13	7	8	43	8
Fodder scam (Lalu Prasad Yadav)	2	4	7	12	8	33	9
Hawala scandal (Hasan Ali)	-	6	15	9	19	49	5
	100	100	100	100	100	500	

Table 9: Your above rating based on

	Frequency	Percent
Personal experience	20	20.0
Other experience	19	19.0
Media	61	61.0

Table 10: Public Interest in Fighting Corruption

Options	n	%	Options	n	%
Interested in fighting corruption			**Corruption as a problem**		
Yes	54	54.0	Local	7	7.0
No	20	20.0	Regional/ District	8	8.0
Not Sure	26	26.0	State	7	7.0
			National	31	31.0
			International	47	47.0

Table 11: Top Reasons of Corruption and Public Ranking

List of reasons for corruption	1	2	3	4	5	Total	Rank
Don't like to spend much time in govt. offices	16	16	16	16	10	74	1
Individual laziness	12	10	21	7	10	60	2
Paid for an illegal work/entity to done	11	5	7	8	7	38	9
Rotten system	10	12	9	11	10	52	3
Do not know the formalities to complain	10	6	8	13	13	50	5
Urgentness of issue	9	10	8	8	9	44	7
Bribe demanding office setup	9	11	5	14	13	52	4
Weak vigilance and anticorruption agency	8	8	12	8	11	47	6
Fearlessness of govt. staff towards the action against corruption	8	5	5	2	9	29	10
Unaware of formalities	4	14	6	12	5	41	8
Low payment to govt. staff	3	3	3	1	3	13	11
	100	100	100	100	100	500	

Table 12: Your above rating based on

	Frequency	Percent
Personal experience	38	38.0
Other experience	25	25.0
Media	37	37.0

Table 13: Appreciating an Act of Corruption by the Participants

During our course of occupation	Yes	No	Not sure
Favoring our neighbors amounts to corruption	73	19	8
Favoring our relatives amounts to corruption	74	20	6
Favoring our best friend amounts to corruption	62	28	10
Using government properties such as using telephone for personnel use will amount to corruption	78	12	10
Using government properties such as using Xerox copier for personnel use will amount to corruption	77	12	11
Using government services such as telephone for personnel use will amount to corruption	79	13	8
Using government properties such as computers for personnel use will amount to corruption	72	21	7
Using government properties such as internet services for personnel use will amount to corruption	74	18	8

Table 14: Respondents Participation in Corruption and Reasons

Options	n	%	Options	n	%
Is bribing a crime			**Bribed for making work done**		
Yes	88	88.0	Yes	68	68.0
No	9	9.0	No	32	32.0
Not Sure	3	3.0	Not Sure	-	-
Was that a demand? (n=68)			**Was that for doing a legal thing/entity (n=68)**		
Yes	35	51.5	Yes	9	13.2
No	26	38.2	No	39	57.4
Not Sure	7	10.3	Not Sure	20	29.4
Interested in complaining the corruption cases			**Would like to be part of social bribing system**		
Yes	56	56.0	Yes	39	39.0
No	31	31.0	No	46	46.0
Not Sure	13	13.0	Not Sure	15	15.0
Support the corruption in public sector			**If yes, can corruption be decriminalize (n=16)**		
Yes	16	16.0	Yes	8	50.0
No	73	73.0	No	7	43.7
Not Sure	11	11.0	Not Sure	1	6.3

Table 15: Participants Experience and Corruption (n= 46)

Was that to achieve following birth rights?	Yes	No	Not sure
For community certificate	35	31	2
For getting driving license	33	35	-
For ration card	31	36	1
For complaint the police station	30	38	-
For birth certificate	27	41	-
For income corticated	25	43	-
For getting scholarship	24	43	1
For getting treatment in government hospitals	23	45	-
For death certificate	21	47	-
For TNGST/CST no	9	59	-

Table 16: Reporting behaviour and Reasons for Not- reporting

Options	Yes	No	Not sure
Attempted to complain on the event of corruption	18	80	2
Seen any officer being bribed	80	20	-
Yes (n=80) Made a complaint to the authorities	18	62	-
Action taken against the complaint (n=18)	6	12	-
Were you happy about the action (n=6)	3	3	-
Rejection of complaint was informed (n=12)	2	10	-
Reason for not reporting the corruption (n=62)			
Unwillingness	38	21	3
Police will act on their own	18	42	2
No faith in police	36	25	1
Don't know whom to report	29	33	-
Fear of reverse action	32	30	-
Problem in witnessing	32	30	-
Fear of police	28	34	-
No action will be taken	39	21	-
Waste of time	46	16	-
Fear/shame	40	21	1

Table 17: Participants Awareness on the Government Measures to Fight Corruption and RTI

Options	Yes	No	Not sure
Aware of department of the vigilance and anti corruption (**V & AC**)?	43	48	9
Aware of the contact address of the office of the V & AC	14	75	11
Aware of the phone numbers of the office of the V & AC?	18	67	15
Aware of the prevention of the corruption act?	**33**	56	11
Does it deal with corruption in public services? **(n=33)**	16	8	9
The Right to Information (RTI) Act, 2005			
Aware of the Right to information (RTI) act, 2005?	30	70	-
The right to information act was enacted to ......? **(n=30)** • To achieve our birth rights.	9	17	4
• To fix accountability and ensure transparency in government working	16	9	5
• T o eliminate corruption and bribe in public bodies.	14	12	4
Ever used RTI? **(n=30)**	4	26	-
Was the attempt a successful one? **(n=4)**	2	2	-
Yes, it was a successful attempt **(n=2)** i. Personal interest and satisfaction	-	1	1
ii. Public cause	1	1	-
iii. Benefit of others	1	1	-

Table 18: Awareness on RTI by the Respondents and their Experience

Options	n	%	Options	n	%
Knowledge of the RTI act, 2005 (n=30)			**Came across success story of winning issues through RTI (n=30)**		
Personnel experience	4	13.3	Yes	14	46.7
Other experience	5	16.7	**Source of knowledge on success stories (14)**		
Media	21	70.0	Personal experience	-	-
			Other experience	5	35.7
			Media	9	64.3

Table 19: Knowledge of Lok Pal and Jan Lok Pal Bill

Options	n	%	Options	n	%
Aware of Lok Pal Bill			**Aware of Jan Lok Pal Bill**		
Yes	48	48.0	Yes	33	33.0
No	50	50.0	No	62	62.0
Not Sure	2	2.0	Not Sure	5	5.0
Lok Pal Empowered with	Yes	Not sure	**Lok Pal Empowered with**	Yes	Not sure
To punish politician	37	3	To punish politician	26	-
To punish state government servant	37	1	To punish state government servant	25	-
To punish central government servant	35	2	To punish central government servant	19	1
To punish all who are corrupt	35	1	To punish all who are corrupt	21	3
To increase the investigation agency's power	25	3	To increase the investigation agency's power	20	3
To control lower level corruption	30	1	To control lower level corruption	20	3
To control higher level corruption	34	2	To control higher level corruption	19	5
To control all forms of corruption	34	4	To control all forms of corruption	22	5

Salem Data- Frequency Tables of the Study

Table 1: Socio-demographic Variables of the Respondents

Options	n	%	Options	n	%
Age in years			**Educational qualification**		
<=20	15	15.0	Until class 10	6	6.0
>20<=30	56	56.0	> 10-12 class	11	11.0
>30<=40	16	16.0	ITI / Dip	-	-
>40	13	13.0	Graduate's and above	75	75.0
Sex			Other specify	8	8.0
Male	50	50.0	**Marital Status**		
Female	50	50.0	Single	70	70.0
Income in Rupees			Married	30	30.0
<=10000	35	35.0	**Family types**		
> 10000 <= 25000	48	48.0	Joint Family	35	35.0
> 25000 <= 50000	15	15.0	Nuclear Family	63	63.0
> 50000	2	2.0	Living Alone	2	2.0

Table 2: The Respondent's and their Father's Occupation

Options	n	%	Options	n	%
Respondent' s occupation			**Father' s occupation**		
Student	46	46.0	Business	8	8.0
Business	-	-	Daily wage labour	13	13.0
Daily wage labour	1	1.0	Govt. employee	23	23.0
Govt. employee	10	10.0	Private employee	10	10.0
Private employee	19	19.0	Home maker	1	1.0
Home maker	11	11.0	Teacher/faculty	3	3.0
Teacher/faculty	3	3.0	Own Profession	12	12.0
Own Profession	7	7.0	Agarian	17	17.0
Agarian	-	-	Retired person	11	11.0
Retired person	3	3.0	Other specify	2	2.0
Other specify	-	-			

Table 3: Public Rating of the Public Sectors with Rank

Rank	1	2	3	4	5	Total	Rank
Register office	32	12	8	4	6	62	2
Police (Crime, traffic, law and order)	14	17	15	17	15	78	1
Revenue department	11	15	11	9	9	55	5
Electricity board (EB)	10	4	4	3	15	36	7
Public distribution system	10	13	11	14	7	55	6
Regional transport office (RTO)	9	19	14	11	6	59	3
Public work department (PWD)	7	10	16	11	12	56	4
Judiciary (Judges/Magistrate, public prosecutor and courts)	3	3	5	9	5	25	9
Government Public Hospitals (GPH)	2	1	10	11	9	33	8
Taxation	2	5	6	5	7	25	10
Trust /Missionaries/ Welfare society/ Ngo's	-	1	-	5	4	10	11
Railways (Indian/Southern any other zonal operator of India)	-	-	-	1	5	6	12
	100	100	100	100	100	500	

Table 4: Basis of the Public Ranking of the Public Sectors and Media Influence

Options	n	%	Options	n	%
Basis of the public rating			**Media influence**		
Personal experience	49	49.0	Yes	37	37.0
Other experience	33	33.0	No	27	27.0
Media	18	18.0	Not Sure	36	36.0

Table 5: Public Interest on Corruption during their Routines

Options	Yes	No	Not sure
Interested in reading the articles published in dailies	61	25	14
Interested in reading the articles published in weeklies	42	37	21
Follow news articles related to corruption on a regular basis	37	45	18
Interested in listening to the news related to corruption in radio	38	45	17
Interested in watching news relating to corruption in television	78	10	12
Followed the articles on corruption published by Wiki leaks	23	62	15
In your opinion do media play a prominent role in whistle blowing?	69	11	20
Media cover only the corruption at higher levels of government?	63	19	18
Media cover only the corruption at local levels of government?	38	34	28

Table 6: Corruption – First Thing that Comes to Participant's Minds

Options	n	%	Options	n	%
Politician	58	58.0	**Above experienced is based on**		
Government sector	39	39.0	Personal experience	20	20.0
Private offices/companies/ schools	3	3.0	Other experience	19	19.0
			Media	58	58.0
			Other Specify	3	3.0

Table 7: Public Personalities and Corruption – Participant's Opinion

Name of the personality	Corruption committed	Prevent corruption	Not Sure	PO*	OC#	Media Yes	No
Raja	80	1	19	-	15	76	9
KaniMozhi	74	-	26	-	9	80	11
Dayanithi Maran	56	5	39	-	10	76	14
Harshad mehtha	40	4	54	-	9	67	24
Ramalinga Raju	35	4	61	-	13	63	24
Prasad bhusan	11	17	72	-	8	61	31
Kiranbedi	9	46	45	-	16	66	18

PO* – Personal opinion

OC# – Other Communication

Table 8: Top Scams and Public Ranking

List of Scams	1	2	3	4	5	Total	Rank
2G Spectrum scam (Raja)	75	7	6	2	4	94	1
Commonwealth games scam (Suresh Kalmadi)	6	28	24	18	9	85	2
IPL Scam (Lalit Modi)	5	19	19	12	17	72	3
Bofors scam (Congress)	3	17	14	6	10	50	4
Insurance fraud (Harshad Mehta Ketan)	3	12	11	12	7	45	5
Satyam Scam (Ramalinga Raju)	3	3	7	14	6	33	9
Hawala scandal (Hasan Ali)	3	3	2	9	17	34	8
Stamp paper scam (Telgi)	2	6	4	11	12	35	7
Stock market scam (Parekh)	-	3	2	6	5	16	10
Fodder scam (Lalu Prasad Yadav)	-	2	11	10	13	36	6
	100	100	100	100	100	500	

Table 9: Your above Rating based on

	Frequency	Percent
Personal experience	16	16.0
Other experience	9	9.0
Media	75	75.0

Table 10: Public Interest in Fighting Corruption

Options	n	%	Options	n	%
Interested in fighting corruption			**Corruption as a problem**		
Yes	57	57.0	Local	1	1.0
No	17	17.0	Regional/ District	1	1.0
Not Sure	26	26.0	State	5	5.0
			National	29	29.0
			International	64	64.0

Table 11: Top Reasons of Corruption and Public Ranking

List of reasons for corruption	1	2	3	4	5	Total	Rank
Paid for an illegal work/entity to done	25	16	15	7	2	65	2
Bribe demanding office setup	25	18	11	11	6	71	1
Weak vigilance and anticorruption agency	10	2	12	17	8	49	5
Urgentness of issue	9	9	11	10	18	57	4
Don' t like to spend much time in govt. offices	8	7	6	13	14	48	6
Rotten system	6	6	8	6	15	41	7
Fearlessness of govt. staff towards the action against corruption	6	10	10	7	5	38	9
Individual laziness	6	14	18	6	20	64	3
Do not know the formalities to complain	4	11	6	14	6	41	8
Low payment to govt. staff	1	3	1	3	2	10	11
Unaware of formalities	-	4	2	6	4	16	10
	100	100	100	100	100	500	

Table 12: Your above rating based on

	Frequency	Percent
Personal experience	43	43.0
Other experience	36	36.0
Media	21	21.0

Table 13: Appreciating an Act of Corruption by the Participants

During our course of occupation	Yes	No	Not sure
Favoring our neighbors amounts to corruption	65	24	11
Favoring our relatives amounts to corruption	69	16	15
Favoring our best friend amounts to corruption	63	23	14
Using government properties such as using telephone for personnel use will amount to corruption	68	19	13
Using government properties such as using Xerox copier for personnel use will amount to corruption	69	13	18
Using government services such as telephone for personnel use will amount to corruption	67	16	17
Using government properties such as computers for personnel use will amount to corruption	66	19	15
Using government properties such as internet services for personnel use will amount to corruption	73	13	14

Table 14: Respondents Participation in Corruption and Reasons

Options	n	%	Options	n	%
Is bribing a crime			**Bribed for making work done**		
Yes	96	96.0	Yes	52	52.0
No	1	1.0	No	40	40.0
Not Sure	3	3.0	Not Sure	8	8.0
Was that a demand? (n=52)			**Was that for doing a legal thing/entity (n=52)**		
Yes	41	78.9	Yes	3	5.8
No	6	11.5	No	37	71.2
Not Sure	5	9.6	Not Sure	12	23.0
Interested in complaining the corruption cases			**Would like to be part of social bribing system**		
Yes	55	55.0	Yes	33	33.0
No	21	21.0	No	43	43.0
Not Sure	24	24.0	Not Sure	24	24.0
Support the corruption in public sector			**If yes, can corruption be decriminalize (n=16)**		
Yes	16	16.0	Yes	5	31.3
No	60	60.0	No	9	56.2
Not Sure	24	24.0	Not Sure	2	12.5

Table 15: Respondents Experience and Corruption (n= 46)

Was that to achieve following birth rights?	Yes	No	Not sure
For community certificate	27	22	3
For getting driving license	21	30	1
For income corticated	17	35	-
For getting treatment in government hospitals	15	37	-
For ration card	12	38	2
For getting scholarship	11	41	-
For birth certificate	10	40	2
For death certificate	9	41	2
For complaint the police station	7	44	1
For TNGST/CST no	4	48	-

Table 16: Reporting behaviour and Reasons for Not- reporting

Options	Yes	No	Not sure
Attempted to complain on the event of corruption	10	89	1
Seen any officer being bribed	72	24	4
Yes (n=72) Made a complaint to the authorities	8	64	-
Action taken against the complaint (n=8)	5	3	-
Were you happy about the action (n=5)	3	1	1
Rejection of complaint was informed(n=3)	-	3	-
Reason for not reporting the corruption (n=64)			
Unwillingness	19	36	9
Police will act on their own	13	44	7
No faith in police	23	37	4
Don't know whom to report	29	32	3
Fear of reverse action	25	35	4
Problem in witnessing	28	32	4
Fear of police	28	33	3
No action will be taken	48	12	4
Waste of time	32	30	2
Fear/shame	27	32	5

Table 17: Participants Awareness on the Government Measures to Fight Corruption and RTI

Options	Yes	No	Not sure
Aware of department of the vigilance and anti corruption (V & AC)?	73	26	1
Aware of the contact address of the office of the V & AC	10	58	5
Aware of the phone numbers of the office of the V & AC?	8	85	7
Aware of the prevention of the corruption act?	35	56	9
Does it deal with corruption in public services? (n=35)	9	14	12
The Right to Information (RTI) Act, 2005			
Aware of the Right to information (RTI) act, 2005?	38	62	-
The right to information act was enacted to ......? (n=38) • To achieve our birth rights.	19	8	11
• To fix accountability and ensure transparency in government working	28	4	6
• T o eliminate corruption and bribe in public bodies.	21	9	8
Ever used RTI? (n=38)	8	30	-
Was the attempt a successful one? (n=8)	3	1	4
Yes, it was a successful attempt (n=5) i. Personal interest and satisfaction	1	2	2
ii. Public cause	3	2	-
iii. Benefit of others	4	1	-

Table 18: Awareness on RTI by the Respondents and their Experience

Options	n	%	Options	n	%
Knowledge of the RTI act, 2005 (n= 38)			**Came across success story of winning issues through RTI (n=38)**		
Personnel experience	1	2.6	Yes	28	73.7
Other experience	15	39.5	**Source of knowledge on success stories (n=28)**		
Media	22	57.9	Personal experience	1	3.6
			Other experience	18	64.3
			Media	9	32.1

Table 19: Knowledge of Lok Pal and Jan Lok Pal Bill

Options	n	%	Options	n	%
Aware of Lok Pal Bill			**Aware of Jan Lok Pal Bill**		
Yes	57	57.0	Yes	33	33.0
No	31	31.0	No	53	53.0
Not Sure	12	12.0	Not Sure	14	14.0
Lok Pal Empowered with	Yes	Not sure	**Lok Pal Empowered with**	Yes	Not sure
To punish politician	45	7	To punish politician	30	5
To punish state government servant	34	17	To punish state government servant	26	8
To punish central government servant	37	11	To punish central government servant	26	9
To punish all who are corrupt	38	11	To punish all who are corrupt	26	8
To increase the investigation agency's power	26	17	To increase the investigation agency's power	23	7
To control lower level corruption	29	19	To control lower level corruption	24	8
To control higher level corruption	34	15	To control higher level corruption	25	10
To control all forms of corruption	38	13	To control all forms of corruption	28	7

ANNEXURE VIII

Tirunelveli Data- Frequency Tables of the Study

Table 1: Socio-demographic Variables of the Respondents

Options	n	%	Options	n	%
Age in years			**Educational qualification**		
<=20	5	5.0	Until class 10	11	11.0
>20<=30	52	52.0	> 10-12 class	16	16.0
>30<=40	22	22.0	ITI / Dip	5	5.0
>40	21	21.0	Graduate's and above	63	63.0
Sex			Other specify	5	5.0
Male	59	59.0	**Marital Status**		
Female	41	41.0	Single	49	49.0
Income in Rupees			Married	50	50.0
<=10000	44	44.0	Divorced	1	1.0
> 10000 <= 25000	39	39.0	**Family types**		
> 25000 <= 50000	14	14.0	Joint Family	27	27.0
> 50000	3	3.0	Nuclear Family	69	69.0
			Living Alone	3	3.0
			Other specify	1	1.0

Table 2: The Respondent's and their Father's Occupation

Options	n	%	Options	n	%
Respondent' s occupation			**Father' s occupation**		
Student	24	24.0	Business	13	13.0
Business	3	3.0	Daily wage labour	16	16.0
Daily wage labour	10	10.0	Govt. employee	21	21.0
Govt. employee	11	11.0	Private employee	11	11.0
Private employee	18	18.0	Home maker	1	1.0
Home maker	13	13.0	Teacher/faculty	1	1.0
Teacher/faculty	-	-	Own Profession	8	8.0
Own Profession	11	11.0	Agarian	10	10.0
Agarian	3	3.0	Retired person	12	12.0
Retired person	3	3.0	Other specify	7	7.0
Other specify	4	4.0			

Table 3: Public Rating of the Public Sectors with Rank

Rank	1	2	3	4	5	Total	Rank
Police (Crime, traffic, law and order)	31	14	16	18	8	87	1
Public distribution system	12	12	13	11	12	60	3
Public work department (PWD)	12	14	13	11	10	60	4
Government Public Hospitals (GPH)	11	8	5	8	2	34	8
Regional transport office (RTO)	9	12	16	14	10	61	2
Register office	8	12	11	12	13	56	5
Revenue department	8	15	11	8	11	53	6
Electricity board (EB)	5	5	5	9	11	35	7
Judiciary (Judges/Magistrate, public prosecutor and courts)	3	6	4	4	7	24	9
Taxation	1	-	6	5	11	23	10
Trust /Missionaries/ Welfare society/ Ngo's	-	-	-	-	2	2	12
Railways (Indian/Southern any other zonal operator of India)	-	2	-	-	3	5	11

Table 4: Basis of the Public Ranking of the Public Sectors and Media Influence

Options	n	%	Options	n	%
Basis of the public rating			**Media influence**		
Personal experience	56	56.0	Yes	52	52.0
Other experience	32	32.0	No	23	23.0
Media	12	12.0	Not Sure	25	25.0

Table 5: Public Interest on Corruption during their Routines

Options	Yes	No	Not sure
Interested in reading the articles published in dailies	58	29	13
Interested in reading the articles published in weeklies	40	43	17
Follow news articles related to corruption on a regular basis	35	42	23
Interested in listening to the news related to corruption in radio	32	48	20
Interested in watching news relating to corruption in television	82	10	8
Followed the articles on corruption published by Wiki leaks	22	62	16
In your opinion do media play a prominent role in whistle blowing?	90	5	5
Media cover only the corruption at higher levels of government?	66	15	19
Media cover only the corruption at local levels of government?	37	25	38

Table 6: Corruption – First thing that comes to Participant's Minds

Options	n	%	Options	n	%
Politician	57	57.0	**Above experienced is based on**		
Government sector	43	43.0	Personal experience	29	29.0
Private offices/ companies/ schools	-	-	Other experience	14	14.0
			Media	57	57.0
			Other Specify	-	-

Table 7: Public Personalities and Corruption – Participant's Opinion

Name of the personality	Corruption committed	Prevent corruption	Not Sure	How did you know			
				PO*	OC#	Media	
						Yes	No
Raja	91	-	9	-	5	86	9
KaniMozhi	82	1	17	-	6	81	13
Dayanithi Maran	62	1	37	-	4	71	25
Ramalinga Raju	34	4	62	-	5	56	39
Harshad mehtha	33	6	61	-	4	56	40
Kiranbedi	16	35	49	-	3	61	36
Prasad bhusan	14	8	78	-	5	49	46

PO* – Personal opinion

OC# – Other Communication

Table 8: Top Scams and Public Ranking

List of Scams	1	2	3	4	5	Total	Rank
2G Spectrum scam (Raja)	76	10	5	2	4	97	1
Bofors scam (Congress)	5	5	7	8	6	31	9
Stamp paper scam (Telgi)	5	3	7	6	13	34	6
Commonwealth games scam (Suresh Kalmadi)	4	47	21	10	6	88	2
Satyam Scam (Ramalinga Raju)	4	10	11	17	7	49	4
Insurance fraud (Harshad Mehta Ketan)	2	1	11	9	11	34	7
IPL Scam (Lalit Modi)	2	15	24	21	14	76	3
Fodder scam (Lalu Prasad Yadav)	2	2	10	6	12	32	8
Stock market scam (Parekh)	-	3	3	11	7	24	10
Hawala scandal (Hasan Ali)	-	4	1	10	20	35	5
	100	100	100	100	100	500	

Table 9: Your above Rating Based on

	Frequency	Percent
Personal experience	8	8.0
Other experience	7	7.0
Media	85	85.0

Table 10: Public Interest in Fighting Corruption

Options	n	%	Options	n	%
Interested in fighting corruption			Corruption as a problem		
Yes	61	61.0	Local	1	
No	22	22.0	Regional/ District	2	
Not Sure	17	17.0	State	7	
			National	23	
			International	67	

Table 11: Top Reasons of Corruption and Public Ranking

List of reasons for corruption	1	2	3	4	5	Total	Rank
Don't like to spend much time in govt. offices	23	15	12	10	10	70	2
Individual laziness	19	12	15	9	15	70	3
Fearlessness of govt. staff towards the action against corruption	11	6	8	7	11	43	5
Weak vigilance and anticorruption agency	10	3	9	9	11	42	6
Paid for an illegal work/entity to done	10	10	9	3	5	37	7
Urgentness of issue	8	13	19	24	13	77	1
Bribe demanding office setup	7	8	4	7	9	35	9
Rotten system	6	15	13	9	7	50	4
Do not know the formalities to complain	2	7	4	14	9	36	8
Unaware of formalities	2	7	5	7	7	28	10
Low payment to govt. staff	2	4	2	1	3	12	11
	100	100	100	100	100	500	

Table 12: Your above Rating Based on

Options	n	%
Personal experience	49	49.0
Other experience	29	29.0
Media	22	22.0

Table 13: Appreciating an Act of Corruption by the Participants

During our course of occupation	Yes	No	Not sure
Favoring our neighbors amounts to corruption	74	23	3
Favoring our relatives amounts to corruption	73	21	6
Favoring our best friend amounts to corruption	67	26	7
Using government properties such as using telephone for personnel use will amount to corruption	80	13	7
Using government properties such as using Xerox copier for personnel use will amount to corruption	83	12	5
Using government services such as telephone for personnel use will amount to corruption	79	14	7
Using government properties such as computers for personnel use will amount to corruption	74	14	12
Using government properties such as internet services for personnel use will amount to corruption	77	13	10

Table 14: Respondent's Participation in Corruption, Sharing and Reasons

Options	n	%	Options	n	%
Is bribing a crime			**Bribed for making work done**		
Yes	99	99.0	Yes	58	58.0
No	1	1.0	No	38	38.0
Not Sure	-	-	Not Sure	4	4.0
Was that a demand? (n=58)			**Was that for doing a legal thing/entity (n=58)**		
Yes	54	93.1	Yes	8	13.8
No	4	6.9	No	38	65.5
Not Sure	-	-	Not Sure	12	20.7
Interested in complaining the corruption cases			**Would like to be part of social bribing system**		
Yes	47	47.0	Yes	33	33.0
No	30	30.0	No	49	49.0
Not Sure	23	23.0	Not Sure	18	18.0
Support the corruption in public sector			**If yes, can corruption be decriminalize (n=15)**		
Yes	15	15.0	Yes	7	46.7
No	68	68.0	No	7	46.7
Not Sure	17	17.0	Not Sure	1	6.6

Table 15: Respondents Experience and Corruption (n= 58)

Was that to achieve following birth rights?	Yes	No	Not sure
For getting driving license	38	18	2
For community certificate	34	20	4
For income corticated	31	23	4
For ration card	25	27	6
For birth certificate	23	29	6
For complaint the police station	23	29	6
For death certificate	22	29	7
For getting treatment in government hospitals	19	35	4
For getting scholarship	7	44	7
For TNGST/CST no	6	43	9

Table 16: Reporting behaviour and Reasons for Not- reporting

Options	Yes	No	Not sure
Attempted to complain on the event of corruption	10	86	4
Seen any officer being bribed	70	18	12
Yes (n=70) Made a complaint to the authorities	8	62	
Action taken against the complaint (n=8)	1	7	-
Were you happy about the action (n=1)	-	1	-
Rejection of complaint was informed(n=7)	1	6	-
Reason for not reporting the corruption (n=62)			
Unwillingness	31	25	6
Police will act on their own	10	35	17
No faith in police	29	24	9
Don't know whom to report	26	28	8
Fear of reverse action	26	27	9
Problem in witnessing	29	25	8
Fear of police	28	28	6
No action will be taken	49	4	9
Waste of time	44	13	5
Fear/shame	21	30	11

Table 17: Participants Awareness on the Government Measures to Fight Corruption and RTI

Options	Yes	No	Not sure
Aware of department of the vigilance and anti corruption (V & AC)?	79	18	3
Aware of the contact address of the office of the V & AC	19	76	5
Aware of the phone numbers of the office of the V & AC?	12	85	3
Aware of the prevention of the corruption act?	34	52	14
Does it deal with corruption in public services? (n=34)	7	14	13
The Right to Information (RTI) Act, 2005			
Aware of the Right to information (RTI) act, 2005?	43	54	3
The right to information act was enacted to ......? (n=43) • To achieve our birth rights.	26	12	5
• To fix accountability and ensure transparency in government working	38	3	2
• T o eliminate corruption and bribe in public bodies.	28	10	5
Ever used RTI? (n=43)	3	40	-
Was the attempt a successful one? (n=3)	2	1	-
Yes, it was a successful attempt (n=1) • Personal interest and satisfaction	1	-	-
• Public cause	-	-	1
• Benefit of others	-	-	1

Table 18: Awareness on RTI by the Respondents and their Experience

Options	n	%	Options	n	%
Knowledge of the RTI act, 2005 (n=43)			**Came across success story of winning issues through RTI (n=43)**		
Personnel experience	3	7.0	Yes	26	60.5
Other experience	20	46.5	**Source of knowledge on success stories (n=26)**		
Media	20	46.5	Personal experience	1	3.9
			Other experience	20	76.9
			Media	5	19.2

Table 19: Knowledge of Lok Pal and Jan Lok Pal Bill

Options	n	%	Options	n	%
Aware of Lok Pal Bill			**Aware of Jan Lok Pal Bill**		
Yes	49	48.0	Yes	53	53.0
No	33	33.0	No	30	30.0
Not Sure	18	19.0	Not Sure	17	17.0
Lok Pal Empowered with	**Yes**	**Not sure**	**Lok Pal Empowered with**	**Yes**	**Not sure**
To punish politician	39	4	To punish politician	48	3
To punish state government servant	31	13	To punish state government servant	37	9
To punish central government servant	28	14	To punish central government servant	37	9
To punish all who are corrupt	29	8	To punish all who are corrupt	45	4
To increase the investigation agency's power	20	10	To increase the investigation agency's power	41	5
To control lower level corruption	31	8	To control lower level corruption	43	3
To control higher level corruption	26	9	To control higher level corruption	43	3
To control all forms of corruption	31	7	To control all forms of corruption	47	3

ANNEXURE IX

Tiruppur Data- Frequency tables of the study

Table 1: Socio-demographic Variables of the Respondents

Options	n	%	Options	n	%
Age in years			**Educational qualification**		
<=20	5	5.0	Until class 10	9	9.0
>20<=30	48	48.0	> 10-12 class	15	15.0
>30<=40	27	27.0	ITI / Dip	3	3.0
>40	20	20.0	Graduate's and above	69	69.0
Sex			Other specify	4	4.0
Male	62	62.0	**Marital Status**		
Female	38	38.0	Single	48	48.0
Income in Rupees			Married	52	52.0
<=10000	37	37.0	**Family types**		
> 10000 <= 25000	42	42.0	Joint Family	35	35.0
> 25000 <= 50000	19	19.0	Nuclear Family	61	61.0
> 50000	2	2.0	Living Alone	4	4.0

Table 2: The Respondent's and their Father's Occupation

Options	n	%	Options	n	%
Respondent' s occupation			**Father' s occupation**		
Student	28	28.0	Business	12	12.0
Business	-	-	Daily wage labour	14	14.0
Daily wage labour	5	5.0	Govt. employee	18	18.0
Govt. employee	6	6.0	Private employee	10	10.0
Private employee	33	33.0	Home maker	3	3.0
Home maker	12	12.0	Teacher/faculty	2	2.0
Teacher/faculty	2	2.0	Own Profession	12	12.0
Own Profession	6	6.0	Agarian	10	10.0
Agarian	1	1.0	Retired person	12	12.0
Retired person	6	6.0	Other specify	7	7.0
Other specify	1	1.0			

Table 3: Public Rating of the Public Sectors with Rank

Rank	1	2	3	4	5	Total	Rank
Police (Crime, traffic, law and order)	27	15	14	17	7	80	1
Register office	17	11	16	10	9	63	2
Regional transport office (RTO)	13	12	11	16	6	58	3
Public distribution system	12	13	9	9	14	57	4
Revenue department	8	12	13	8	9	50	5
Government Public Hospitals (GPH)	7	3	11	8	7	36	8
Electricity board (EB)	4	9	2	13	14	42	7
Judiciary (Judges/Magistrate, public prosecutor and courts)	4	6	4	8	2	24	9
Public work department (PWD)	3	12	12	8	15	50	6
Taxation	3	5	6	2	3	19	10
Railways (Indian/Southern any other zonal operator of India)	2	-	1	1	6	10	12
Trust /Missionaries/ Welfare society/ Ngo's	-	2	1	-	8	11	11
	100	100	100	100	100		

Table 4: Basis of the Public Ranking of the Public Sectors and Media Influence

Options	n	%	Options	n	%
Basis of the public rating			**Media influence**		
Personal experience	51	51.0	Yes	53	53.0
Other experience	30	30.0	No	21	21.0
Media	19	19.0	Not Sure	26	26.0

Table 5: Public Interest on Corruption during their Routines

Options	Yes	No	Not sure
Interested in reading the articles published in dailies	74	18	8
Interested in reading the articles published in weeklies	50	36	14
Follow news articles related to corruption on a regular basis	47	39	14
Interested in listening to the news related to corruption in radio	42	49	9
Interested in watching news relating to corruption in television	77	16	7
Followed the articles on corruption published by Wiki leaks	23	56	21
In your opinion do media play a prominent role in whistle blowing?	79	9	12
Media cover only the corruption at higher levels of government?	60	19	21
Media cover only the corruption at local levels of government?	32	36	32

Table 6: Corruption – First thing that Comes to Participant's Minds

Options	n	%	Options	n	%
Politician	56	56.0	**Above experienced is based on**		
Government sector	43	43.0	Personal experience	26	26.0
Private offices/ companies/ schools	1	1.0	Other experience	17	17.0
			Media	56	56.0
			Other Specify	1	1.0

Table 7: Public Personalities and Corruption – Participants Opinion

Name of the personality	Corruption committed	Prevent corruption	Not Sure	How did you know			
				PO*	OC#	Media	
						Yes	No
Raja	89	2	9	1	10	81	8
KaniMozhi	86	1	13	-	10	80	10
Dayanithi Maran	64	4	32	-	7	75	18
Ramalinga Raju	43	3	54	1	5	68	26
Harshad mehtha	39	7	54	1	6	65	28
Prasad bhusan	13	19	68	1	5	61	33
Kiranbedi	8	41	51	1	7	58	34

PO* – Personal opinion

OC# – Other Communication

Table 8: Top Scams and Public Ranking

List of Scams	1	2	3	4	5	Total	Rank
2G Spectrum scam (Raja)	67	11	4	2	7	91	1
Commonwealth games scam (Suresh Kalmadi)	8	36	16	15	7	82	2
Bofors scam (Congress)	7	9	11	10	10	47	4
Satyam Scam (Ramalinga Raju)	4	7	14	14	8	47	5
Stamp paper scam (Telgi)	4	4	5	13	14	40	7
IPL Scam (Lalit Modi)	3	17	27	15	12	74	3
Insurance fraud (Harshad Mehta Ketan)	2	7	14	7	12	42	6
Stock market scam (Parekh)	2	3	-	4	6	15	10
Fodder scam (Lalu Prasad Yadav)	2	1	9	10	13	35	8
Hawala scandal (Hasan Ali)	1	5	-	10	11	27	9
	100	100	100	100	100		

Table 9: Your Above Rating Based on

	Frequency	Percent
Personal experience	11	11.0
Other experience	12	12.0
Media	77	77.0

Table 10: Public Interest in Fighting Corruption

Options	n	%	Options	n	%
Interested in fighting corruption			Corruption as a problem		
Yes	59	59.0	Local	1	1.0
No	17	17.0	Regional/ District	2	2.0
Not Sure	24	24.0	State	5	5.0
			National	35	35.0
			International	57	57.0

Table 11: Top Reasons of Corruption and Public Ranking

List of reasons for corruption	1	2	3	4	5	Total	Rank
Individual laziness	20	11	9	3	16	59	3
Paid for an illegal work/entity to done	17	13	14	9	6	59	4
Don't like to spend much time in govt. offices	15	9	13	11	11	59	5
Bribe demanding office setup	13	19	8	13	8	61	1
Weak vigilance and anticorruption agency	12	4	7	12	11	46	6
Rotten system	8	10	11	8	9	46	7
Urgentness of issue	8	13	9	16	14	60	2
Do not know the formalities to complain	4	8	8	11	9	40	9
Fearlessness of govt. staff towards the action against corruption	3	7	14	10	9	43	8
Unaware of formalities	-	4	5	6	6	21	10
Low payment to govt. staff	-	2	2	1	1	6	11
	100	100	100	100	100		

Table 12: Your above Rating Based on

	Frequency	Percent
Personal experience	44	44.0
Other experience	31	31.0
Media	25	25.0

Table 13: Appreciating an Act of Corruption by the Participants

During our course of occupation	Yes	No	Not sure
Favoring our neighbors amounts to corruption	76	16	8
Favoring our relatives amounts to corruption	75	15	10
Favoring our best friend amounts to corruption	70	15	15
Using government properties such as using telephone for personnel use will amount to corruption	77	15	8
Using government properties such as using Xerox copier for personnel use will amount to corruption	76	15	9
Using government services such as telephone for personnel use will amount to corruption	63	18	19
Using government properties such as computers for personnel use will amount to corruption	67	20	13
Using government properties such as internet services for personnel use will amount to corruption	71	15	14

Table 14: Respondents Participation in Corruption, Sharing and Reasons

Options	n	%	Options	n	%
Is bribing a crime			**Bribed for making work done**		
Yes	97	97.0	Yes	57	57.0
No	2	2.0	No	36	36.0
Not Sure	1	1.0	Not Sure	7	7.0
Was that a demand? (n=57)			**Was that for doing a legal thing/entity (n=57)**		
Yes	45	79.0	Yes	11	19.3
No	8	14.0	No	33	57.9
Not Sure	4	7.0	Not Sure	13	22.8
Interested in complaining the corruption cases			**Would like to be part of social bribing system**		
Yes	60	60.0	Yes	41	41.0
No	21	21.0	No	40	40.0
Not Sure	19	19.0	Not Sure	19	19.0
Support the corruption in public sector			**If yes, can corruption be decriminalize (n=16)**		
Yes	16	16.0	Yes	5	31.2
No	67	67.0	No	9	56.3
Not Sure	17	17.0	Not Sure	2	12.5

Table 15: Respondents Experience and Corruption (n= 57)

Was that to achieve following birth rights?	Yes	No	Not sure
For getting driving license	30	25	2
For community certificate	29	23	5
For income corticated	25	29	3
For death certificate	20	29	8
For birth certificate	19	32	6
For ration card	18	33	6
For complaint the police station	18	35	4
For getting treatment in government hospitals	17	36	4
For getting scholarship	12	39	6
For TNGST/CST no	10	42	5

Table 16: Reporting behaviour and Reasons for Not- reporting

Options	Yes	No	Not sure
Attempted to complain on the event of corruption	11	87	2
Seen any officer being bribed	77	15	8
Yes **(n=77)** Made a complaint to the authorities	8	69	-
Action taken against the complaint **(n=8)**	3	5	-
Were you happy about the action **(n=3)**	2	1	-
Rejection of complaint was informed**(n=5)**	1	4	-
Reason for not reporting the corruption (n=69)			
Unwillingness	31	28	10
Police will act on their own	12	43	14
No faith in police	35	24	10
Don't know whom to report	33	26	10
Fear of reverse action	29	30	10
Problem in witnessing	29	29	11
Fear of police	26	32	11
No action will be taken	42	15	12
Waste of time	47	15	7
Fear/shame	26	26	17

Table 17: Participants Awareness on the Government Measures to Fight Corruption and RTI

Options	Yes	No	Not sure
Aware of department of the vigilance and anti corruption (V & AC)?	76	19	5
Aware of the contact address of the office of the V & AC	17	78	5
Aware of the phone numbers of the office of the V & AC?	14	81	5
Aware of the prevention of the corruption act?	25	58	17
Does it deal with corruption in public services? (n=25)	6	8	11
The Right to Information (RTI) Act, 2005			
Aware of the Right to information (RTI) act, 2005?	40	60	-
The right to information act was enacted to ......? (n=40) • To achieve our birth rights.	24	10	6
• To fix accountability and ensure transparency in government working	37	1	2
• T o eliminate corruption and bribe in public bodies.	27	7	6
Ever used RTI? (n=40)	9	31	-
Was the attempt a successful one? (n=9)	4	2	3
Yes, it was a successful attempt (n=5) i. Personal interest and satisfaction	2	3	-
ii. Public cause	3	1	1
iii. Benefit of others	3	1	1

Table 18: Awareness on RTI by the Respondents and their Experience

Options	n	%	Options	n	%
Knowledge of the RTI act, 2005 (n=40)			**Came across success story of winning issues through RTI (n= 40)**		
Personnel experience	1	2.5	Yes	24	60.0
Other experience	19	47.5	**Source of knowledge on success stories (n=24)**		
Media	20	50.0	Personal experience	3	12.5
			Other experience	11	45.8
			Media	10	41.7

Table 19: Knowledge of Lok Pal and Jan Lok Pal Bill

Options	n	%	Options	n	%
Aware of Lok Pal Bill			**Aware of Jan Lok Pal Bill**		
Yes	62	62.0	Yes	47	47.0
No	26	26.0	No	41	41.0
Not Sure	12	12.0	Not Sure	12	12.0
Lok Pal Empowered with	**Yes**	**Not sure**	**Lok Pal Empowered with**	**Yes**	**Not sure**
To punish politician	50	7	To punish politician	42	3
To punish state government servant	44	8	To punish state government servant	34	8
To punish central government servant	36	10	To punish central government servant	35	8
To punish all who are corrupt	37	9	To punish all who are corrupt	41	5
To increase the investigation agency's power	40	9	To increase the investigation agency's power	39	3
To control lower level corruption	42	6	To control lower level corruption	39	6
To control higher level corruption	41	8	To control higher level corruption	37	7
To control all forms of corruption	44	8	To control all forms of corruption	42	4

Trichy Data- Frequency Tables of the Study

Table 1: Socio-demographic Variables of the respondents

Options	n	%	Options	n	%
Age in years			**Educational qualification**		
<=20	20	20.0	Until class 10	3	3.0
>20<=30	21	21.0	> 10-12 class	24	24.0
>30<=40	35	35.0	ITI / Dip	4	4.0
>40	24	24.0	Graduate's and above	67	67.0
Sex			Other specify	2	2.0
Male	49	49.0	**Marital Status**		
Female	51	51.0	Single	40	40.0
Income in Rupees			Married	55	55.0
<=10000	57	57.0	Divorced	2	2.0
> 10000 <= 25000	30	30.0	Widow	3	3.0
> 25000 <= 50000	10	10.0	**Family types**		
> 50000	3	3.0	Joint Family	40	40.0
			Nuclear Family	56	56.0
			Living Alone	4	4.0

Table 2: The Respondent's and their father's Occupation

Options	n	%	Options	n	%
Respondent' s occupation			**Father' s occupation**		
Student	21	21.0	Business	17	17.0
Business	4	4.0	Daily wage labour	12	12.0
Daily wage labour	6	6.0	Govt. employee	10	10.0
Govt. employee	21	21.0	Private employee	11	11.0
Private employee	25	25.0	Home maker	1	1.0
Home maker	4	4.0	Teacher/faculty	2	2.0
Teacher/faculty	10	10.0	Own Profession	4	4.0
Own Profession	6	6.0	Agarian	28	28.0
Agarian	2	2.0	Retired person	11	11.0
Retired person	-	-	Other specify	4	4.0
Other specify	1	1.0			

Table 3: Public Rating of the Public Sectors with Rank

Rank	1	2	3	4	5	Total	Rank
Revenue department	32	16	9	5	6	68	2
Public work department (PWD)	21	22	7	7	8	65	3
Register office	15	17	5	2	3	42	6
Police (Crime, traffic, law and order)	14	7	26	28	7	82	1
Regional transport office (RTO)	4	10	8	4	9	35	7
Electricity board (EB)	3	3	6	4	10	26	9
Taxation	3	6	8	5	8	30	8
Railways (Indian/Southern any other zonal operator of India)	3	-	2	2	10	17	10
Government Public Hospitals (GPH)	2	2	4	19	20	47	5
Public distribution system	2	13	24	11	9	59	4
Judiciary (Judges/Magistrate, public prosecutor and courts)	1	4	1	6	3	15	11
Trust /Missionaries/ Welfare society/ Ngo's	-	-	-	7	7	14	12
	100	100	100	100	100	500	

Table 4: Basis of the Public Ranking of the Public Sectors and Media Influence

Options	n	%	Options	n	%
Basis of the public rating			**Media influence**		
Personal experience	51	51.0	Yes	46	46.0
Other experience	31	31.0	No	26	26.0
Media	18	18.0	Not Sure	28	28.0

Table 5: Public Interest on Corruption during their Routines

Options	Yes	No	Not sure
Interested in reading the articles published in dailies	69	19	12
Interested in reading the articles published in weeklies	43	43	14
Follow news articles related to corruption on a regular basis	39	48	13
Interested in listening to the news related to corruption in radio	29	58	13
Interested in watching news relating to corruption in television	63	18	19
Followed the articles on corruption published by Wiki leaks	32	40	28
In your opinion do media play a prominent role in whistle blowing?	77	6	17
Media cover only the corruption at higher levels of government?	44	27	29
Media cover only the corruption at local levels of government?	37	17	46

Table 6: Corruption – First thing that Comes to Participant's Minds

Options	n	%	Options	n	%
Politician	75	75.0	**Above experienced is based on**		
Government sector	25	25.0	Personal experience	16	16.0
Private offices/ companies/ schools	-	-	Other experience	9	9.0
			Media	75	75.0

Table 7: Public Personalities and Corruption – Participant's Opinion

Name of the personality	Corruption committed	Prevent corruption	Not Sure	How did you know			
				PO*	OC#	Media	
						Yes	No
Raja	89	-	11	-	5	87	8
KaniMozhi	74	-	26	-	5	78	17
Ramalinga Raju	57	7	36	-	8	64	28
Dayanithi Maran	56	1	43	-	5	66	29
Harshad mehtha	41	7	52	-	6	58	36
Prasad bhusan	30	15	55	-	6	54	40
Kiranbedi	9	63	28	-	6	75	19

PO* – Personal opinion

OC# – Other Communication

Table 8: Top Scams and Public Ranking

List of Scams	1	2	3	4	5	Total	Rank
2G Spectrum scam (Raja)	61	13	11	5	5	95	1
IPL Scam (Lalit Modi)	14	15	19	19	11	78	3
Bofors scam (Congress)	11	14	8	5	4	42	6
Hawala scandal (Hasan Ali)	5	7	2	11	30	55	5
Commonwealth games scam (Suresh Kalmadi)	3	26	30	13	7	79	2
Stamp paper scam (Telgi)	3	10	11	26	8	58	4
Stock market scam (Parekh)	1	-	2	2	3	8	10
Satyam Scam (Ramalinga Raju)	1	6	8	10	9	34	7
Fodder scam (Lalu Prasad Yadav)	1	2	4	5	16	28	8
Insurance fraud (Harshad Mehta Ketan)	-	7	5	4	7	23	9
	100	100	100	100	100	500	

Table 9: Your above Rating based on

Options	Frequency	Percent
Personal experience	8	8.0
Other experience	13	13.0
Media	79	79.0

Table 10: Public Interest in Fighting Corruption

Options	n	%	Options	n	%
Interested in fighting corruption			**Corruption as a problem**		
Yes	71	71.0	Regional/ District	-	-
No	13	13.0	State	3	3.0
Not Sure	16	16.0	National	40	40.0
			International	57	57.0

Table 11: Top Reasons of Corruption and Public Ranking

List of reasons for corruption	1	2	3	4	5	Total	Rank
Urgentness of issue	26	15	17	9	4	71	1
Rotten system	15	11	10	3	9	48	6
Don't like to spend much time in govt. offices	13	14	13	9	13	62	2
Paid for an illegal work/entity to done	9	5	6	11	8	39	8
Weak vigilance and anticorruption agency	8	8	12	11	6	45	7
Fearlessness of govt. staff towards the action against corruption	8	8	7	8	3	34	9
Bribe demanding office setup	7	9	4	15	15	50	5
Do not know the formalities to complain	6	13	12	18	7	56	3
Individual laziness	4	12	8	4	28	56	4
Low payment to govt. staff	3	1	4	2	2	12	11
Unaware of formalities	1	4	7	10	5	27	10
	100	100	100	100	100	500	

Table 12: Your Above Rating based on

	Frequency	Percent
Personal experience	36	36.0
Other experience	36	36.0
Media	28	28.0

Table 13: Appreciating an Act of Corruption by the Participants

During our course of occupation	Yes	No	Not sure
Favoring our neighbors amounts to corruption	65	29	6
Favoring our relatives amounts to corruption	64	25	11
Favoring our best friend amounts to corruption	63	27	10
Using government properties such as using telephone for personnel use will amount to corruption	75	11	14
Using government properties such as using Xerox copier for personnel use will amount to corruption	75	7	18
Using government services such as telephone for personnel use will amount to corruption	80	7	13
Using government properties such as computers for personnel use will amount to corruption	79	7	14
Using government properties such as internet services for personnel use will amount to corruption	82	3	15

Table 14: Respondents Participation in Corruption and Reasons

Options	n	%	Options	n	%
Is bribing a crime			**Bribed for making work done**		
Yes	98	98.0	Yes	53	53.0
No	-	-	No	43	43.0
Not Sure	2	2.0	Not Sure	4	4.0
Was that a demand? (n=53)			**Was that for doing a legal thing/entity (n=53)**		
Yes	39	73.6	Yes	1	1.9
No	12	22.6	No	40	75.5
Not Sure	2	3.8	Not Sure	12	22.6
Interested in complaining the corruption cases			**Would like to be part of social bribing system**		
Yes	73	73.0	Yes	27	27.0
No	16	16.0	No	42	42.0
Not Sure	11	11.0	Not Sure	31	31.0
Support the corruption in public sector			**If yes, can corruption be decriminalize (n=10)**		
Yes	10	10.0	Yes	5	50.0
No	59	59.0	No	4	40.0
Not Sure	31	31.0	Not Sure	1	10.0

Table 15: Respondents Experience and Corruption (n= 53)

Was that to achieve following birth rights?	Yes	No	Not sure
For getting driving license	38	15	-
For community certificate	31	20	2
For birth certificate	26	26	1
For income corticated	26	26	1
For ration card	20	32	1
For death certificate	18	34	1
For complaint the police station	15	36	2
For getting treatment in government hospitals	14	38	1
For getting scholarship	8	45	47
For TNGST/CST no	6	46	1

Table 16: Reporting behaviour and Reasons for Not-reporting

Options	Yes	No	Not sure
Attempted to complain on the event of corruption	10	90	-
Seen any officer being bribed	69	29	2
Yes (n= 69) Made a complaint to the authorities	10	59	-
Action taken against the complaint (n=10)	3	6	1
Were you happy about the action (n=3)	-	3	-
Rejection of complaint was informed (n=7)	2	5	-
Reason for not reporting the corruption (n=72)			
Unwillingness	29	25	5
Police will act on their own	18	36	5
No faith in police	22	34	3
Don't know whom to report	21	35	3
Fear of reverse action	31	25	3
Problem in witnessing	28	28	3
Fear of police	21	33	5
No action will be taken	38	18	3
Waste of time	34	23	2
Fear/shame	27	27	5

Table 17: Participants Awareness on the Government Measures to Fight Corruption and RTI

Options	Yes	No	Not sure
Aware of department of the vigilance and anti corruption (V & AC)?	84	16	-
Aware of the contact address of the office of the V & AC	27	66	7
Aware of the phone numbers of the office of the V & AC?	18	74	8
Aware of the prevention of the corruption act?	41	47	12
Does it deal with corruption in public services? (n=41)	8	14	19
The Right to Information (RTI) Act, 2005			
Aware of the Right to information (RTI) act, 2005?	37	62	1
The right to information act was enacted to ……? (n=37) • To achieve our birth rights.	16	14	7
• To fix accountability and ensure transparency in government working	31	4	2
• T o eliminate corruption and bribe in public bodies.	20	11	6
Ever used RTI? (n=37)	7	30	-
Was the attempt a successful one? (n=7)	3	4	-
Yes, it was a successful attempt (n=4) • Personal interest and satisfaction	4	-	-
• Public cause	1	3	-
• Benefit of others	1	3	-

Table 18: Awareness on RTI by the Respondents and their Experience

Options	n	%	Options	n	%
Knowledge of the RTI act, 2005 (n=37)			**Came across success story of winning issues through RTI (n=62.2)**		
Personnel experience	2	5.4	Yes	23	23.0
Other experience	17	45.9	**Source of knowledge on success stories (n=23)**		
Media	18	48.7	Personal experience	2	8.7
			Other experience	15	65.2
			Media	6	26.1

Table 19: Knowledge of Lok Pal and Jan Lok Pal Bill

Options	n	%	Options	n	%
Aware of Lok Pal Bill			**Aware of Jan Lok Pal Bill**		
Yes	45	45.0	Yes	38	38.0
No	44	44.0	No	49	49.0
Not Sure	11	11.0	Not Sure	13	13.0
Lok Pal Empowered with	**Yes**	**Not sure**	**Lok Pal Empowered with**	**Yes**	**Not sure**
To punish politician	36	3	To punish politician	27	3
To punish state government servant	29	8	To punish state government servant	23	4
To punish central government servant	29	7	To punish central government servant	25	4
To punish all who are corrupt	37	6	To punish all who are corrupt	27	2
To increase the investigation agency's power	24	7	To increase the investigation agency's power	24	5
To control lower level corruption	25	11	To control lower level corruption	23	4
To control higher level corruption	30	7	To control higher level corruption	27	4
To control all forms of corruption	34	7	To control all forms of corruption	29	3

Annexure XI

Tuticorn Data- Frequency Tables of the Study

Table 1: Socio-demographic Variables of the Respondents

Options	n	%	Options	n	%
Age in years			**Educational qualification**		
<=20	6	6.0	Until class 10	4	4.0
>20<=30	52	52.0	> 10-12 class	11	11.0
>30<=40	28	28.0	ITI / Dip	10	10.0
>40	14	14.0	Graduate's and above	70	70.0
Sex			Other specify	5	5.0
Male	63	63.0	**Marital Status**		
Female	37	37.0	Single	52	52.0
Income in Rupees			Married	48	48.0
<=10000			**Family types**		
> 10000 <= 25000			Joint Family	32	32.0
> 25000 <= 50000			Nuclear Family	63	63.0
> 50000			Living Alone	5	5.0

Table 2: The Respondent's and their Father's Occupation

Options	n	%	Options	n	%
Respondent' s occupation			**Father' s occupation**		
Student	36	36.0	Business	11	11.0
Business	1	1.0	Daily wage labour	16	16.0
Daily wage labour	6	6.0	Govt. employee	19	19.0
Govt. employee	4	4.0	Private employee	11	11.0
Private employee	36	36.0	Home maker	2	2.0
Home maker	7	7.0	Teacher/faculty	3	3.0
Teacher/faculty	3	3.0	Own Profession	14	14.0
Own Profession	1	1.0	Agarian	8	8.0
Agarian	1	1.0	Retired person	7	7.0
Retired person	2	2.0	Other specify	9	9.0
Other specify	3	3.0			

Table 3: Public Rating of the Public Sectors with Rank

Rank	1	2	3	4	5	Total	Rank
Police (Crime, traffic, law and order)	25	17	12	12	5	71	1
Regional transport office (RTO)	14	12	10	8	5	49	4
Revenue department	12	20	12	14	10	68	3
Public work department (PWD)	9	6	3	7	13	38	7
Register office	9	16	23	10	12	70	2
Judiciary (Judges/Magistrate, public prosecutor and courts)	7	2	3	10	5	27	10
Electricity board (EB)	6	7	8	14	6	41	6
Government Public Hospitals (GPH)	6	6	9	6	10	37	8
Public distribution system	4	9	7	12	16	48	5
Taxation	4	4	9	4	10	31	9
Railways (Indian/Southern any other zonal operator of India)	3	-	-	1	2	6	12
Trust /Missionaries/ Welfare society/ Ngo's	1	1	4	2	6	14	11
	100	100	100	100	100		

Table 4: Basis of the Public Ranking of the Public Sectors and Media Influence

Options	n	%	Options	n	%
Basis of the public rating			**Media influence**		
Personal experience	57	57.0	Yes	49	49.0
Other experience	20	20.0	No	26	26.0
Media	23	23.0	Not Sure	25	25.0

Table 5: Public Interest on Corruption during their Routines

Options	Yes	No	Not sure
Interested in reading the articles published in dailies	75	16	9
Interested in reading the articles published in weeklies	48	36	16
Follow news articles related to corruption on a regular basis	49	34	17
Interested in listening to the news related to corruption in radio	50	39	11
Interested in watching news relating to corruption in television	79	12	9
Followed the articles on corruption published by Wiki leaks	32	41	27
In your opinion do media play a prominent role in whistle blowing?	76	14	10
Media cover only the corruption at higher levels of government?	60	21	19
Media cover only the corruption at local levels of government?	34	43	23

Table 6: Corruption – First thing that Comes to Participant's Minds

Options	n	%	Options	n	%
Politician	69	69.0	**Above experienced is based on**		
Government sector	31	31.0	Personal experience	19	19.0
Private offices/companies/ schools	-	-	Other experience	12	12.0
			Media	69	69.0

Table 7: Public Personalities and Corruption – Participants Opinion

Name of the personality	Corruption committed	Prevent corruption	Not Sure	How did you know			
				PO*	OC#	Media	
						Yes	No
Raja	83	-	17	-	14	72	14
KaniMozhi	83	-	17	-	14	71	15
Dayanithi Maran	74	-	26	-	13	65	22
Ramalinga Raju	59	3	38	-	12	57	31
Harshad mehtha	52	6	42	-	11	52	37
Prasad bhusan	19	26	55	-	10	50	40
Kiranbedi	12	54	34	-	11	58	31

PO* – Personal opinion

OC# – Other Communication

Table 8: Top Scams and Public Ranking

List of Scams	1	2	3	4	5	Total	Rank
2G Spectrum scam (Raja)	77	9	2	-	3	91	1
Bofors scam (Congress)	10	27	9	9	4	59	4
Commonwealth games scam (Suresh Kalmadi)	3	19	37	12	9	80	2
IPL Scam (Lalit Modi)	3	12	11	17	27	70	3
Stock market scam (Parekh)	2	2	-	7	5	16	10
Satyam Scam (Ramalinga Raju)	2	17	9	17	9	54	5
Stamp paper scam (Telgi)	2	2	4	9	11	28	8
Hawala scandal (Hasan Ali)	1	6	1	8	10	26	9
Insurance fraud (Harshad Mehta Ketan)	-	5	15	11	10	41	6
Fodder scam (Lalu Prasad Yadav)	-	1	12	10	12	35	7
	100	100	100	100	100		

Table 9: Your above Rating based on

	Frequency	Percent
Personal experience	18	18.0
Other experience	10	10.0
Media	72	72.0

Table 10: Public Interest in Fighting Corruption

Options	n	%	Options	n	%
Interested in fighting corruption			Corruption as a problem		
Yes	65	65.0	Regional/ District	3	3.0
No	19	19.0	State	4	4.0
Not Sure	16	16.0	National	50	50.0
			International	43	43.0

Table 11: Top Reasons of Corruption and Public Ranking

List of reasons for corruption	1	2	3	4	5	Total	Rank
Don' t like to spend much time in govt. offices	19	13	13	8	7	60	2
Individual laziness	17	10	10	9	16	62	1
Paid for an illegal work/entity to done	16	8	14	10	5	53	4
Urgentness of issue	12	14	12	13	8	59	3
Rotten system	11	8	12	7	10	48	7
Weak vigilance and anticorruption agency	8	10	10	13	9	50	6
Fearlessness of govt. staff towards the action against corruption	7	7	8	11	11	44	8
Do not know the formalities to complain	3	3	7	10	13	36	9
Bribe demanding office setup	3	20	9	10	11	53	5
Low payment to govt. staff	2	-	3	2	6	13	11
Unaware of formalities	1	8	2	7	4	22	10
	100	101	100	100	100		

Table 12: Your above Rating Based on

	Frequency	Percent
Personal experience	45	45.0
Other experience	21	21.0
Media	34	34.0

Table 13: Appreciating an Act of Corruption by the Participants

During our course of occupation	Yes	No	Not sure
Favoring our neighbors amounts to corruption	70	16	14
Favoring our relatives amounts to corruption	69	15	16
Favoring our best friend amounts to corruption	65	18	17
Using government properties such as using telephone for personnel use will amount to corruption	69	13	18
Using government properties such as using Xerox copier for personnel use will amount to corruption	71	13	16
Using government services such as telephone for personnel use will amount to corruption	62	13	25
Using government properties such as computers for personnel use will amount to corruption	61	17	22
Using government properties such as internet services for personnel use will amount to corruption	62	14	24

Table 14: Respondents Participation in Corruption, Sharing and Reasons

Options	n	%	Options	n	%
Is bribing a crime			**Bribed for making work done**		
Yes	96	96.0	Yes	67	67.0
No	3	3.0	No	23	23.0
Not Sure	1	1.0	Not Sure	10	10.0
Was that a demand? (n=67)			**Was that for doing a legal thing/entity (n=67)**		
Yes	52	77.6	Yes	12	17.9
No	10	14.9	No	37	55.2
Not Sure	5	7.5	Not Sure	18	26.9
Interested in complaining the corruption cases			**Would like to be part of social bribing system**		
Yes	65	65.0	Yes	43	43.0
No	23	23.0	No	31	31.0
Not Sure	12	12.0	Not Sure	26	26.0
Support the corruption in public sector			**If yes, can corruption be decriminalize (n=16)**		
Yes	16	16.0	Yes	5	31.2
No	60	60.0	No	10	62.5
Not Sure	24	24.0	Not Sure	1	6.3

Table 15: Respondents Experience and Corruption (n= 67)

Was that to achieve following birth rights?	Yes	No	Not sure
For getting driving license	39	26	2
For community certificate	37	27	3
For income corticated	32	32	3
For birth certificate	31	33	3
For getting treatment in government hospitals	29	34	4
For death certificate	27	35	5
For complaint the police station	26	40	1
For ration card	23	37	7
For TNGST/CST no	16	48	3
For getting scholarship	13	47	7

Table 16: Reporting behaviour and Reasons for Not- Reporting

Options	Yes	No	Not sure
Attempted to complain on the event of corruption	8	92	-
Seen any officer being bribed	76	19	5
Yes (n=76) Made a complaint to the authorities	8	68	-
Action taken against the complaint (n=8)	4	4	-
Were you happy about the action (n=4)	1	3	-
Rejection of complaint was informed (n=4)	-	3	1
Reason for not reporting the corruption (n=68)			
Unwillingness	27	35	6
Police will act on their own	7	52	9
No faith in police	28	31	9
Don't know whom to report	30	33	5
Fear of reverse action	31	33	4
Problem in witnessing	29	34	5
Fear of police	25	36	7
No action will be taken	43	20	5
Waste of time	44	16	8
Fear/shame	20	35	13

Table 17: Participants Awareness on the Government Measures to Fight Corruption and RTI

Options	Yes	No	Not sure
Aware of department of the vigilance and anti corruption (V & AC)?	74	21	5
Aware of the contact address of the office of the V & AC	24	74	2
Aware of the phone numbers of the office of the V & AC?	17	81	2
Aware of the prevention of the corruption act?	29	66	5
Does it deal with corruption in public services? (n=29)	12	6	11
The Right to Information (RTI) Act, 2005			
Aware of the Right to information (RTI) act, 2005?	42	58	-
The right to information act was enacted to ......? (n=42) • To achieve our birth rights.	27	11	4
• To fix accountability and ensure transparency in government working	38	1	3
• T o eliminate corruption and bribe in public bodies.	25	7	10
Ever used RTI? (n=42)	13	29	-
Was the attempt a successful one? (n=13)	5	4	4
Yes, it was a successful attempt (n=8) • Personal interest and satisfaction	2	6	-
• Public cause	5	3	-
• Benefit of others	5	3	-

Table 18: Awareness on RTI by the Respondents and their Experience

Options	n	%	Options	n	%
Knowledge of the RTI act, 2005 **(n= 42)**			**Came across success story of winning issues through RTI** **(n=42)**		
Personnel experience	4	9.5	Yes	29	69.0
Other experience	13	31.0	**Source of knowledge on success stories (n=29)**		
Media	25	59.5	Personal experience	4	13.8
			Other experience	19	65.5
			Media	6	20.7

Table 19: Knowledge of Lok Pal and Jan Lok Pal Bill

Options	n	%	Options	n	%
Aware of Lok Pal Bill			**Aware of Jan Lok Pal Bill**		
Yes	57	57.0	Yes	54	54.0
No	27	27.0	No	30	30.0
Not Sure	16	16.0	Not Sure	16	16.0
Lok Pal Empowered with	**Yes**	**Not sure**	**Lok Pal Empowered with**	**Yes**	**Not sure**
To punish politician	47	5	To punish politician	41	8
To punish state government servant	43	8	To punish state government servant	35	9
To punish central government servant	41	8	To punish central government servant	37	9
To punish all who are corrupt	46	2	To punish all who are corrupt	46	3
To increase the investigation agency's power	37	9	To increase the investigation agency's power	38	8
To control lower level corruption	35	9	To control lower level corruption	40	8
To control higher level corruption	42	5	To control higher level corruption	39	9
To control all forms of corruption	47	3	To control all forms of corruption	48	5

Vellore Data- Frequency Tables of the Study

Table 1: Socio-demographic Variables of the Respondents

Options	n	%	Options	n	%
Age in years			**Educational qualification**		
<=20	6	6.0	Until class 10	9	9.0
>20<=30	59	59.0	> 10-12 class	13	13.0
>30<=40	22	22.0	ITI / Dip	7	7.0
>40	13	13.0	Graduate's and above	71	71.0
Sex			Other specify	-	-
Male	67	67.0	**Marital Status**		
Female	33	33.0	Single	58	58.0
Income in Rupees			Married	42	42.0
<=10000	58	58.0	**Family types**		
> 10000 <= 25000	27	27.0	Joint Family	33	33.0
> 25000 <= 50000	9	9.0	Nuclear Family	64	64.0
> 50000	6	6.0	Living Alone	2	2.0
			Other specify	1	1.0

Table 2: The Respondent's and their Father's Occupation

Options	n	%	Options	n	%
Respondent' s occupation			**Father' s occupation**		
Student	49	49.0	Business	10	10.0
Business	3	3.0	Daily wage labour	21	21.0
Daily wage labour	12	12.0	Govt. employee	20	20.0
Govt. employee	12	12.0	Private employee	16	16.0
Private employee	9	9.0	Home maker	1	1.0
Home maker	9	9.0	Teacher/faculty	-	-
Teacher/faculty	-	-	Own Profession	6	6.0
Own Profession	2	2.0	Agarian	18	18.0
Agarian	3	3.0	Retired person	5	5.0
Retired person	-	-	Other specify	3	3.0
Other specify	1	1.0			

Table 3: Public Rating of the Public Sectors with Rank

Rank	1	2	3	4	5	Total	Rank
Police (Crime, traffic, law and order)	31	13	9	21	11	85	1
Register office	16	11	23	10	9	69	2
Public work department (PWD)	13	16	11	8	12	60	4
Public distribution system	9	16	13	15	15	68	3
Railways (Indian/Southern any other zonal operator of India)	7	-	3	8	6	24	8
Regional transport office (RTO)	6	8	17	7	11	49	6
Revenue department	6	17	9	13	9	54	5
Judiciary (Judges/Magistrate, public prosecutor and courts)	5	3	3	3	5	19	10
Taxation	4	6	5	2	7	24	9
Government Public Hospitals (GPH)	2	7	3	8	7	27	7
Electricity board (EB)	1	2	3	4	8	18	11
Trust /Missionaries/ Welfare society/ Ngo's	-	1	1	1	-	3	12

Table 4: Basis of the Public Ranking of the Public Sectors and Media Influence

Options	n	%	Options	n	%
Basis of the public rating			**Media influence**		
Personal experience	43	43.0	Yes	58	58.0
Other experience	37	37.0	No	16	16.0
Media	20	20.0	Not Sure	26	26.0

Table 5: Public Interest on Corruption during their Routines

Options	Yes	No	Not sure
Interested in reading the articles published in dailies	63	24	13
Interested in reading the articles published in weeklies	32	53	15
Follow news articles related to corruption on a regular basis	39	46	15
Interested in listening to the news related to corruption in radio	32	58	10
Interested in watching news relating to corruption in television	75	12	13
Followed the articles on corruption published by Wiki leaks	24	59	17
In your opinion do media play a prominent role in whistle blowing?	78	3	19
Media cover only the corruption at higher levels of government?	64	13	23
Media cover only the corruption at local levels of government?	52	22	26

Table 6: Corruption – First thing that Comes to Participant's Minds

Options	n	%	Options	n	%
Politician	72	72.0	**Above experienced is based on**		
Government sector	18	18.0	Personal experience	16	16.0
Private offices/companies/ schools	-	-	Other experience	12	12.0
			Media	72	72.0
			Other Specify	-	-

Table 7: Public Personalities and Corruption – Participant's Opinion

Name of the personality	Corruption committed	Prevent corruption	Not Sure	How did you know			
				PO*	OC#	Media	
						Yes	No
Raja	88	-	12	-	1	88	11
KaniMozhi	74	-	26	-	1	79	20
Harshad mehtha	51	1	48	-	1	59	40
Dayanithi Maran	51	1	47	-	1	70	29
Ramalinga Raju	49	-	51	-	-	61	39
Prasad bhusan	11	23	66	-	1	52	47
Kiranbedi	10	39	51	-	-	63	37

PO* – Personal opinion

OC# – Other Communication

Table 8: Top Scams and Public Ranking

List of Scams	1	2	3	4	5	Total	Rank
2G Spectrum scam (Raja)	84	5	3	2	1	95	1
Bofors scam (Congress)	4	22	3	10	9	48	5
IPL Scam (Lalit Modi)	4	9	26	18	18	75	3
Commonwealth games scam (Suresh Kalmadi)	3	29	37	13	9	91	2
Stamp paper scam (Telgi)	2	5	8	8	17	40	7
Fodder scam (Lalu Prasad Yadav)	2	5	3	6	9	25	8
Satyam Scam (Ramalinga Raju)	1	8	6	16	19	50	4
Insurance fraud (Harshad Mehta Ketan)	-	7	8	19	8	42	6
Stock market scam (Parekh)	-	5	3	3	6	17	9
Hawala scandal (Hasan Ali)	-	5	3	5	4	17	10
	100	100	100	100	100	500	

Table 9: Your Above Rating based on

	Frequency	Percent
Personal experience	4	4.0
Other experience	7	7.0
Media	89	89.0

Table 10: Public Interest in Fighting Corruption

Options	n	%	Options	n	%
Interested in fighting corruption			Corruption as a problem		
Yes	50	50.0	Regional/ District	-	-
No	22	22.0	State	5	5.0
Not Sure	28	28.0	National	34	34.0
			International	61	61.0

Table 11: Top Reasons of Corruption and Public Ranking

List of reasons for corruption	1	2	3	4	5	Total	Rank
Urgentness of issue	19	11	17	11	10	68	1
Bribe demanding office setup	18	9	7	7	12	53	5
Don' t like to spend much time in govt. offices	14	13	14	13	14	68	2
Paid for an illegal work/entity to done	13	15	14	8	10	60	3
Weak vigilance and anticorruption agency	10	9	9	14	3	45	6
Individual laziness	10	11	12	12	13	58	4
Rotten system	5	7	5	9	5	31	9
Do not know the formalities to complain	5	6	6	6	16	39	8
Low payment to govt. staff	3	2	3	5	5	18	
Fearlessness of govt. staff towards the action against corruption	3	12	9	10	8	42	7
Unaware of formalities	-	5	4	5	4	18	10

Table 12: Your above Rating based on

Options	n	%
Personal experience	26	26.0
Other experience	47	47.0
Media	27	27.0

Table 13: Appreciating an Act of Corruption by the Participants

During our course of occupation	Yes	No	Not sure
Favoring our neighbors amounts to corruption	68	20	12
Favoring our relatives amounts to corruption	72	17	11
Favoring our best friend amounts to corruption	68	21	11
Using government properties such as using telephone for personnel use will amount to corruption	74	17	9
Using government properties such as using Xerox copier for personnel use will amount to corruption	71	19	10
Using government services such as telephone for personnel use will amount to corruption	72	18	10
Using government properties such as computers for personnel use will amount to corruption	69	21	10
Using government properties such as internet services for personnel use will amount to corruption	73	17	10

Table 14: Respondents Participation in Corruption and Reasons

Options	n	%	Options	n	%
Is bribing a crime			**Bribed for making work done**		
Yes	96	96.0	Yes	49	49.0
No	-	-	No	36	36.0
Not Sure	4	4.0	Not Sure	15	15.0
Was that a demand? (n=49)			**Was that for doing a legal thing/entity (n=49)**		
Yes	40	81.6	Yes	4	8.2
No	4	8.2	No	24	48.9
Not Sure	5	10.2	Not Sure	21	42.9
Interested in complaining the corruption cases			**Would like to be part of social bribing system**		
Yes	48	48.0	Yes	26	26.0
No	31	31.0	No	48	48.0
Not Sure	21	21.0	Not Sure	26	26.0
Support the corruption in public sector			**If yes, can corruption be decriminalize (n=18)**		
Yes	18	18.0	Yes	5	27.8
No	66	66.0	No	9	50.0
Not Sure	16	16.0	Not Sure	4	22.0

Table 15: Respondents Experience and Corruption (n= 49)

Was that to achieve following birth rights?	Yes	No	Not sure
For community certificate	27	21	1
For income corticated	25	22	2
For getting driving license	24	24	1
For birth certificate	17	30	2
For ration card	14	35	-
For complaint the police station	14	31	4
For death certificate	13	34	2
For getting treatment in government hospitals	12	33	4
For getting scholarship	11	35	3
For TNGST/CST no	5	41	3

Table 16: Reporting behaviour and Reasons for Not-reporting

Options	Yes	No	Not sure
Attempted to complain on the event of corruption	11	85	4
Seen any officer being bribed	72	13	15
Yes (n=72) Made a complaint to the authorities	13	59	-
Action taken against the complaint (n=13)	2	6	5
Were you happy about the action (n=2)	2	-	-
Rejection of complaint was informed (n=11)	-	11	-
Reason for not reporting the corruption (n=59)			
Unwillingness	25	31	3
Police will act on their own	8	47	4
No faith in police	18	36	5
Don't know whom to report	15	40	4
Fear of reverse action	23	33	3
Problem in witnessing	22	35	2
Fear of police	20	35	4
No action will be taken	24	32	3
Waste of time	33	25	1
Fear/shame	26	27	6

Table 17: Participants Awareness on the Government Measures to Fight Corruption and RTI

Options	Yes	No	Not sure
Aware of department of the vigilance and anti corruption (V & AC)?	71	23	6
Aware of the contact address of the office of the V & AC	24	71	5
Aware of the phone numbers of the office of the V & AC?	19	77	4
Aware of the prevention of the corruption act?	37	53	10
Does it deal with corruption in public services? (n=37)	10	14	13
The Right to Information (RTI) Act, 2005			
Aware of the Right to information (RTI) act, 2005?	40	60	-
The right to information act was enacted to ......? (n=40) • To achieve our birth rights.	31	2	7
• To fix accountability and ensure transparency in government working	32	1	7
• T o eliminate corruption and bribe in public bodies.	23	4	13
Ever used RTI? (n=40)	13	27	-
Was the attempt a successful one? (n=13)	7	5	1
Yes, it was a successful attempt (n=6) • Personal interest and satisfaction	2	4	-
• Public cause	5	1	-
• Benefit of others	5	1	-

Table 18: Awareness on RTI by the Respondents and their Experience

Options	n	%	Options	n	%
Knowledge of the RTI act, 2005 (n=40)			**Came across success story of winning issues through RTI (n=40)**		
Personnel experience	6	15.0	Yes	26	65.0
Other experience	20	50.0	**Source of knowledge on success stories (n=26)**		
Media	14	35.0	Personal experience	4	15.4
			Other experience	15	57.7
			Media	7	26.9

Table 19: Knowledge of Lok Pal and Jan Lok Pal Bill

Options	n	%	Options	n	%
Aware of Lok Pal Bill			**Aware of Jan Lok Pal Bill**		
Yes	62	62.0	Yes	49	49.0
No	15	15.0	No	23	23.0
Not Sure	23	23.0	Not Sure	28	28.0
Lok Pal Empowered with	**Yes**	**Not sure**	**Lok Pal Empowered with**	**Yes**	**Not sure**
To punish politician	47	9	To punish politician	41	4
To punish state government servant	36	11	To punish state government servant	40	4
To punish central government servant	31	14	To punish central government servant	42	3
To punish all who are corrupt	32	15	To punish all who are corrupt	39	3
To increase the investigation agency's power	22	24	To increase the investigation agency's power	36	8
To control lower level corruption	30	17	To control lower level corruption	35	8
To control higher level corruption	29	19	To control higher level corruption	36	9
To control all forms of corruption	35	16	To control all forms of corruption	40	6

Subject Index

www.ingramcontent.com/pod-product-compliance
Lightning Source LLC
Chambersburg PA
CBHW050510160726

48003CB00001B/247